Acclaim for *Throw Out t...*

Survey Comments from Workshop ...

A+ for applicability of content

Very thought provoking

Wonderful, engaging, and educational

So many concrete ideas

Very practical and easy to implement

Excellent and interesting

Good tools

Relevant and executable

Will be able to take these ideas and implement them immediately

Very practical and helpful

Excited to go back and apply what I learned

Inspired me

Good ideas and clarity

Great, enthusiastic, implementable suggestions and ideas

Best practice guidance on a very challenging strategic HR issue

Wow! The content is great!

Loved more innovative way to approach HR issues

Dynamic duo

Something you can walk away with and start using

Absolutely fantastic

Completely relevant to real work

Phenomenal, engaging, humorous, interactive, informative

Loved it!

Throw Out the Ratings

Performance Evaluations that Really Work

Marsha Moulton & William Sparks

Title: Throw Out the Ratings

Subtitle: Performance Evaluations that Really Work

Authors: Marsha Moulton, William Sparks

Published by: Promptitude Publishing in Denton, Maryland

Cover design: William Sparks

Cover images courtesy of www.pixabay.com.

Although based on experience gained working with various employers, in particular ACDI/VOCA, as well as relevant source materials, this publication is solely the work product of its authors, who take full responsibility for its contents. The publication has not been sponsored by any employer or other third party, and the views and concepts expressed in the work does not necessarily represent those of the employers for which the authors have worked.

First Edition, 2017

ISBN # 978-0-692-88986-2

Published in the United States of America

10 9 8 7 6 5 4 3 2 1

*For all employees, past and present,
who have contributed to the mission of ACDI/VOCA*

"The task of leadership is to be intentional
about the way we group people
and the questions that we engage them in."

~Peter Block

"The road to success
is always under construction."

~Lily Tomlin

Table of Contents

About the Authors

Marsha Moulton and William Sparks are recipients of the Dr. J.P. London Award for Promoting Ethical Behavior. Their collaboration in developing the AchieVe performance management system resulted in selection as a finalist for the Human Resources Leadership Award for Innovation. They also received the Operational Excellence Award in 2013 from InsideNGO for their work in performance management. Marsha and William have presented workshops for a variety of organizations, including InsideNGO and the Society for Human Resources Professionals (SHRM) on topics related to performance management, onboarding, leadership, and organizational effectiveness.

Marsha Moulton has over twenty-five years of experience in leading human resources in both for profit and nonprofit environments. Within her roles, she has contributed to developing internal structures that encourage employee empowerment and create a culture that reflects organizations' values. She has designed performance management systems that facilitate staff development and ensure the attainment of organization objectives. Marsha currently serves as the executive vice president for human resources and administration for ACDI/VOCA (www.acdivoca.org), an international organization building social and economic opportunities in over 40 countries. She earned her Master of Science degree in Applied Behavioral Sciences from Johns Hopkins University.

When Marsha is not working, she and her husband Jeff pursue their artistic interests and enjoy traveling. They spend as much time as schedules permit at their second home in the Finger Lakes of New York.

William Sparks has over twenty years of management and international development experience in building organizational capacity throughout Africa, Asia, South America, and Europe. He is the author of *Process Mapping Road Trip: Improve organizational workflow in 5 steps*. His international work includes the creation of Sell More For More, a capacity development program for cooperative organizations in the least developed countries. The program was named a best practice for international development by InterAction and IFAD. He currently serves as senior vice president of strategic initiatives at ACDI/VOCA (www.acdivoca.org), an international organization building social and economic opportunities in over 40 countries. William earned his Master of Science in Organization Development from Pepperdine University.

William, with his wife Jennifer and daughter Vienna, enjoy exploring new cultures. For relaxation, William is an ultra-marathon runner who runs every morning in whichever country he finds himself that day.

Foreword

The phrase, "he or she is ahead of their time," is one I have heard periodically. Rarely can one say they personally know one, let alone two people who personify that phrase. But I do, and this book will let you get to know them, too.

First, let me take you back to 2009. I was searching for organizations in the international development and relief sector who were doing innovative work in performance management. Given global teams, limited resources, and the never-ending litany of dissatisfaction with current annual reviews, I wanted to showcase new approaches at an upcoming annual conference to be hosted by InsideNGO. At that time, there was a lot of discussion about what was not working, but very little about how to change the process. It is then when I connected with Marsha Moulton, one of the authors. She described an initiative that she and William Sparks (author) had introduced to their organization, ACDI/VOCA. It had started off as a small pilot project and had blossomed to a successful initiative that they were happy to share with others in the community. For those that heard that presentation in July 2010, little did they know they were getting a sneak peek into the future.

It would be several more years before revamping of performance management became a hot trend. In the past two to three years, large corporations such as General Electric, Microsoft, Accenture, and the Gap have thrown out their traditional performance reviews. The financial and time cost of this process and its lack of producing desired results have caused these companies and throngs more to pause and revamp. But has it made a difference? And if so, what were the processes that made it successful? While many companies proudly tout that they have tossed their ratings, few share the details of how to successfully make this happen and most have not had enough time to analyze what positive impact changes have made. Gratefully, the approaches shared in this book have been tested by time and their impact measured!

As you read ahead, the experiences of a forward-thinking HR professional are melded together with an innovative, dynamic organizational learning professional to create a recipe of steps, insights, and stories to help you and your organization navigate the reshaping of your performance management.

So, what makes this book different? First, it is fun. Yes, the dreaded topic of performance management is discussed with an honesty and simplicity that energizes you. Second, as you journey through each of the six chapters, your excitement builds as what is laid out before you is a roadmap for rebuilding your internal process. With ten years of practice and refinement, the authors share with you not only what was done but also the "how."

I recall first hearing the term "forward reviews" seven years ago in a presentation by Marsha and William. It seemed novel not to look back at past performance and prior issues ("gotchas") but rather think only about "Now" and "Next." What a different conversation to be having. A staff member sits down to discuss their current goals and their development needs to meet the next set of goals. The supervisor no longer must play statistician pitting team members against each other with ratings, but rather gets to play the role of coach helping the employee be a positive contributor to the overall needs and strategies of the organization. Yes, it was truly a different way of thinking; and while now this conversation has become more mainstream, it is by no means universally done or done well. Emphasizing strengths-based feedback is an empowering conversation. I am sure you will gain some fresh insights as you read more about this.

Working in the non-profit sector for most of my career, the largest asset each organization has is their people. Nothing can be more important than to have engaged and motivated staff who are bringing their "A" game to help deliver on the mission's promise. Without clarity of direction, understanding how one fits into the big picture, coaching for growth and excellence, employees don't excel nor do their organizations. This book serves as a tool to build that engagement through a solid performance management process that throws out the ratings and refocuses on what is important.

While by no means an easy task to transform a process, this book will certainly become a valued guide. I wish you a successful journey as you strive to AchieVe success within your organization.

Marie McNamee

New York, New York

Preface

Our collaborative efforts began in 2006 at ACDI/VOCA. It has been a true equal partnership. We each own our distinct areas of expertise and provide unique contributions to our projects, but we are at our best when we collaboratively pursue answers to vexing workplace challenges. We feel privileged that we can think and create within this complimentary phenomenon.

Combined, we have almost 25 years working at ACDI/VOCA, a not-for-profit economic development organization that fosters broad-based economic growth, raises living standards, and creates vibrant communities in developing countries worldwide. Based in Washington, D.C., ACDI/VOCA has worked in 146 countries since 1963. We brought our knowledge of performance management and organization development to this organization, where we were provided the space to create, develop, and implement a performance management system that was truly a development tool for the organization's employees.

Work on this book was highly dependent on our access to the ACDI/VOCA workplace and our responsibility for ensuring that employees were provided with the best and most advanced performance assessment tools available. This provided us with the opportunity to design a new performance management system firmly grounded in the real-life circumstances of the ACDI/VOCA workplace. Our daily observations of the workplace provided much of the material on which we relied in creating and beta-testing the new system we have named AchieVe. Without the support of ACDI/VOCA in implementing and evaluating, and subsequently in reaching out to other organizations with our system, this book would not have been possible.

We're glad that you've chosen this book to explore a new perspective on performance management. We hope that you enjoy the journey.

Acknowledgments

Marsha & William would like to thank…

- Carl Leonard, Bill Polidoro, and the leadership of ACDI/VOCA for supporting the development and implementation of AchieVe…and for the encouragement to share this experience through workshops and this book.
- Marie McNamee at InsideNGO for her enthusiastic, contagious, sincere, and never ending support for shaping their message and sharing this program with the wider industry. Without those workshops and speaking opportunities, there would be no book.

Marsha would also like to thank…

- Jeff, her spouse and love of her life, for his continual support in everything she does.
- Fran D'Ooge, her mentor who taught her about business and fair practice by living what she advised and didn't give up on her.

William would also like to thank…

- Jennifer, his wife, and Vienna, his daughter, for their continual love, support, and cheers throughout the travel, workshops, and all the drafts of this book.
- The MSOD Community of the Graziadio Business School at Pepperdine University for the long gray line of infinite inspiration, lifelong friendship, and undying commitment to a better world.

Introduction

Pick a Number

Would you stand up in front of a few hundred people in a convention hall and juggle three tennis balls?

This is how we demonstrate that ratings are not helpful.

When we get to this part of our AchieVe workshop, we casually describe that today's professionals are busier than ever. It seems that we are expected to do more and more in the same amount of time. Nonchalantly, we ask members of the audience to raise a hand if they see themselves as an effective multi-tasker—someone who can work on several initiatives simultaneously. Many hands go up in the air.

Now it's time to pick our unsuspecting volunteer.

We call on someone and ask them to come to the stage. After we introduce them to the crowd, we confirm that they believe that they are an effective multi-tasker. They usually nod enthusiastically. We then ask them to demonstrate this critical skill to the audience.

We ask them to juggle three tennis balls as a metaphor for juggling multiple tasks. You can guess what happens next. It doesn't go very well. Some people throw one ball at a time up in the air, catch it, and then throw the next one. Some people dive right in and throw them all, and the dropped balls go bouncing across the stage. The multi-tasker/jugglers are always good sports, but there is definitely no successful juggling.

Now, we are not sure what percentage of the population knows how to juggle. We could guess not a very high percentage, as we've yet to find someone who has met the challenge of juggling. But, the fun part is yet to come.

We turn to the audience of professionals and explain that our multi-tasker is now going to receive a performance review. The performance review is going to be on the single skill of multi-tasking. The audience – who has just witnessed a demonstration of this person's skill – is going to evaluate the performance.

Everyone in the audience has a polling device. It's a small device that looks like a tiny remote control for a television. Our instructions are simple: press 1 if the multi-tasker exceeded expectations, press 2 if the multi-tasker met expectations, and press 3 if the multi-tasker did not meet expectations. This is common performance evaluation language that many people have seen, possibly even on the evaluations in their own company.

What do you think happens next?

Just as often as the multi-tasker fails to juggle the balls, the audience evaluation of the multi-tasker is spread somewhat evenly over the three scores.

What? How can this be? They all saw the same performance! How can everyone evaluate the performance so differently? Aren't we using an objective rating system to give us a clear picture of the person's performance?

In our debrief with the audience, we ask those who selected "3" (did not meet expectations) to explain their choice. They can be summarized as "Duh, the person didn't juggle the balls. Thus, did not meet the expectation of juggling." This seems to be very clear and well-articulated reasoning.

When we ask those who selected "2" (met expectations), they say something similar to "Well, the person did exactly what we expected them to do." So, this seems a fair and reasonable interpretation. Really, what random person at a business conference is going to step up and juggle three balls successfully?

Next we ask those who selected "1" (exceeded expectations). The other members of the audience are quite interested to hear the rationale behind this group. How could someone have exceeded expectations? After all, the multi-tasker didn't even come close to juggling the three tennis balls.

This group explains their rationale like this: "The expectation of an audience member is to come to this event, listen attentively, and take notes. The person who went up on the stage to juggle has far exceeded expectations of what is expected of us." Hmm, another perspective.

Which perspective is right? That's not the point. The point is that all three groups have a valid – but different – opinion of the performance. All three groups have valid rationale; however, all of this is lost in the ratings. In fact, this dispels the notion that ratings are somehow objective. They are not. They are very much influenced by the subjective rationale of the person completing the form.

In statistics, this is called reliability. If different people observe the same event, will they give it the same rating? In our experience with performance reviews that rely primarily on ratings, they are not reliable. Supervisors across an organization do not consistently provide a similar score for similar performance. We're sure that you already know this, and that's why you've picked up this book.

If we can see this much variance in our simple example of multi-tasking, how much more variance will be seen with all the complex skills expected of employees? But reliability isn't the only problem. It isn't even the biggest problem.

The bigger problem is that a rating does not provide guidance for improving performance. Isn't that, after all, why we're going through this process…to help employees improve their performance?

In our simple example, imagine if by some chance the whole audience agreed that the employee was a '2' (met expectations). What does the employee do from here? What did the employee do well, and what needs to be improved? How does the employee walk away from this review with specific, concrete, and tangible ways to improve the skill?

Ratings are not helpful. And, in some cases, they become a distraction. The ratings themselves become the focal point rather than the observations and learning behind the ratings. Employees become more obsessed with getting a higher number than with actually improving a skill. Most frequently, we've seen reviews with a five-point (1-5) rating scale. Even employees that score a '4' will debate as to why they didn't get a '5' on their review.

What a wasted conversation. Wouldn't it be a better conversation to explore the employee's strengths, the value of their contributions to the organization, and ways in which their strengths could be further developed? For a supervisor and an employee, wouldn't both get more value from this deeper dialogue? Ultimately, wouldn't the department and organization benefit more from a focused discussion that aligned the talents of the employee with the objectives of the organization?

That's what this book is about.

We will share with you specific steps for establishing a performance review system that helps employees identify their strengths, gives structure to feedback provided by supervisors, and facilitates a meaningful dialogue to chart a clear path forward.

And, yes, it begins by throwing out the ratings.

Bad Medicine

We were recently at a business cocktail reception, and the conversation turned to our favorite topic: performance management (okay, perhaps we need to get a hobby!). When we explained that we had developed and implemented a performance management system, the VP of an international organization sadly complained that they were in desperate need of a new performance evaluation plan, but he just didn't know where to start. This is the normal reaction we get when we talk to professionals about performance evaluations. It seems that everyone agrees that they don't like their current system, but they either can't agree on what to do or become overwhelmed to the point that they don't know what to do first.

What makes performance evaluations so bad? Depending on your role, you don't like performance evaluations for different reasons. Generally, we all like feedback about ourselves. Few of us can resist the temptation to take an online quiz that compares us to some proverbial average. Yet employees dread being 'judged' by a supervisor and often have difficulty listening to feedback without making a sharp rebuttal. The annual evaluation becomes a heart-thumping face-off where each comment risks becoming a hostile confrontation.

On the flip side, otherwise perfectly rational and self-assured supervisors can crumble at the thought of sitting down with an employee to discuss performance. Often untrained in providing feedback, supervisors either sidestep meaningful feedback that could be helpful to an employee's career or verbally hit them over the head with it. Too often the meeting is focused on the ratings and includes a well-rehearsed argument over a tenth of one percentage point. Supervisors don't see the point of the performance reviews because the process does little to change behavior or help their employees to be more successful.

Conversely, human resources professionals are concerned about documenting performance. They want the process to be legally compliant and to justify promotion and compensation decisions. Mostly, they just want them done and in the file so they can stop badgering supervisors and get on with all their other work. Too often they have given up on the performance evaluation as a meaningful tool that accomplishes anything.

You are not alone in these feelings. Search "employee evaluations" on Amazon books and over *five thousand* titles pop up! The trend is in two directions: more structure or nothing at all. One school of thought is that all you need to do is provide a long enough list of phrases to cover every situation, and the evaluation writes itself. HR software providers see the value in providing these customers with what they want. They support this trend by providing stock phrases to managers and allowing them to assign ratings. This reduces all performance down to a number that categorizes employees and can be aggregated across the organization for ranking purposes. The advantage is that these ready-made evaluations are faster and easier, which appeals to supervisors. HR professionals like them because it requires less training. They can quickly justify personnel actions based on the ratings, and it produces a document (mostly) free of risk.

Ratings also offer another advantage. A movement is underway to make HR more metric focused. The thought is that CEOs understand numbers. If we can reduce our employees to numbers like our financial counterparts, then we may start to speak the same language as our CEO and CFO. Numbers-speak will earn us more respect in the C-Suite.

Based on our research and experience, we have concluded that the single most important step in changing the performance evaluation process is to *eliminate ratings*. No number scale, and certainly no use of vague terms like "satisfactory" or "outstanding" in reviews. By the end of this book, we hope that you join the growing number of professionals who have eliminated ratings in performance evaluations.

The other trend in human resource literature is to eliminate the performance evaluation altogether. After all, it is said, performance reviews are a waste of time and serve no purpose. This solution makes HR professionals nervous. Although they will agree that evaluations in their current state may not serve a purpose connected to staff development, they will also explain that evaluations serve as a justification for compensation and promotion decisions. In fact, most HR literature recommends that the primary elements of an evaluation – feedback and goal-setting – be repackaged as some other process altogether.

Why now?

We agree that performance evaluations as they currently exist in most organizations should be eliminated. We also think that they should be replaced with something that serves as a development tool for employees and aligns their efforts with organizational goals. There is never a bad time to create a performance evaluation system that is a staff development tool, but it may be even more important now.

According to a Pew Research analysis of census data, one in three employees are millennials. Although we do not agree that any generation can be painted with a broad brush, surveys have consistently showed that a large percentage of millennials are very interested in receiving meaningful feedback on a frequent and consistent basis. Further, they are reported to be unlikely to ask for it from their supervisors.

Although the performance management system we are proposing does not include weekly feedback sessions, it is a tool that requires supervisors to provide meaningful feedback. Once your supervisors have become skilled in the AchieVe system, they will increase their ability to provide helpful feedback that many employees crave. It is a short step to the habit of providing such feedback on a regular basis. As the fight for talent continues to heat up, your organization will be in a better position to attract and retain talent from the largest living generation.

Four R's of Performance Management

Why else are performance evaluations so bad? They are designed to predominately look backward and be corrective. That is not inherently a bad thing to do. All professional sports teams review footage of their games to see what they could have done better and learn from their mistakes. It is this *overwhelming* focus on looking backward that hinders future performance. If someone does their job well 95 percent of the time, supervisors can be tempted to place unhelpful emphasis on the remaining five percent of performance. Many supervisors feel pressured to advise employees on how they need to improve to justify their roles as supervisors. "We can all improve, right?" The employee is expected to absorb the advice. The year is over; time to move on.

Perhaps the worst aspect of many reviews is goal-setting. During our years of involvement with performance evaluations, we have read thousands of reviews. Most of them contained de-motivating goals. Goals are generally ignored and often not revisited during the next review to see if they were achieved. Goal writing fails for a variety of reasons. They may be merely a list of tasks lifted right off the job description or describe ambitions not within the control of the employee to achieve. They may be disconnected from any previous performance or completely disconnected from the employee's professional aspirations. Most unfortunately, they are almost always written without any consideration of alignment with the strategic objectives of the organization.

If we are to facilitate the empowerment of employees, then what are the essential elements of a good performance management system? As illustrated below, there are the four R's:

- ***R****each organizational goals.* The fundamental purpose of a performance management system is to achieve organizational goals. Thus, all activities in providing feedback and setting goals must align each employee with overall organizational strategy and objectives.

- ***R****ealize individual growth.* People are motivated by a sense of growth and accomplishment in their jobs. Organizations become stronger when each employee develops or deepens talents and abilities. As individuals increase their ability, so does the collective abilities of the organization.

- ***R****einforce core values.* All companies have stated values, but few systematically reinforce these core values. Examples abound of organizations that have suffered from shady behaviors. Only by reinforcing core values can a culture be strengthened to repel self-destructive activities.

- ***R****etain critical skills.* High turnover can leave some organizations feeling like a university that develops individuals and then sends them out into the marketplace. A sound performance management system identifies the critical skills necessary to achieve sustained organizational success. A clear path for growth ensures the retention of talent.

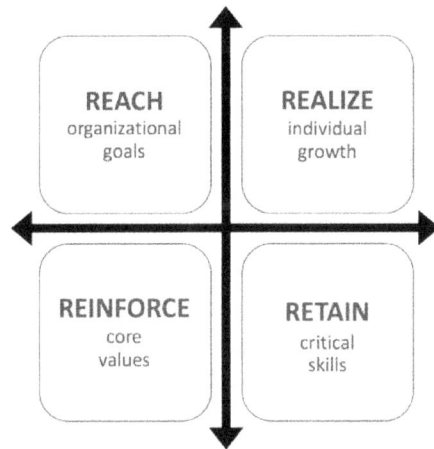

REACH
organizational
goals

REALIZE
individual
growth

REINFORCE
core
values

RETAIN
critical
skills

As you continue leading initiatives to improve your performance management system, we hope you keep these principles in mind as a guide. Further, we find that these principles provide a solid outline for communications to stakeholders. Performance management isn't only an HR concern; it is vital to the success of the entire organization!

Six of One

We developed the six elements of this performance system while working for an international development firm: ACDI/VOCA…or, as we affectionately refer to it internally, A/V. We named our performance management system AchieVe. Hence, the capitalization of the A and V in AchieVe. Of course, you can call your system whatever works for your organization, but we do encourage you to name it.

There are six main elements of the AchieVe performance system, and a chapter has been written for each element. Chapter one defines **Performance Areas**. These will be the foundation of your performance management system. Chapter two replaces ratings and numbers with the **Forward Review**. These two elements are designed to *inform* the employee.

In chapters three and four, we show how the employee shapes professional *intent*. Chapter three describes the process to create compelling **Discipline Goals**. Chapter four defines **Strategy Links** between individual goals and organizational objectives.

The theme of the final chapters is *insight*. In chapter five, we explain how to collect and share information through **Upward Feedback**. All of this comes together with implementation guidance in chapter six, **AchieVe Success**.

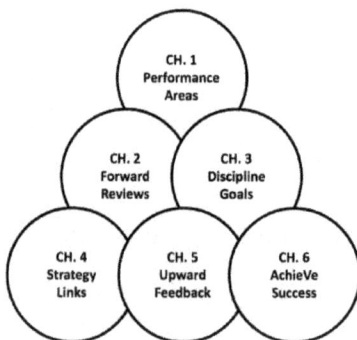

CH. 1
Performance
Areas

CH. 2
Forward
Reviews

CH. 3
Discipline
Goals

CH. 4
Strategy
Links

CH. 5
Upward
Feedback

CH. 6
AchieVe
Success

Each chapter has four specific steps. In general, it is best to read through the chapters in order as they will reference back to earlier elements. However, you can jump directly to a specific chapter if that is an area of immediate concern for you.

So, let's get started…

Chapter 1: Performance Areas

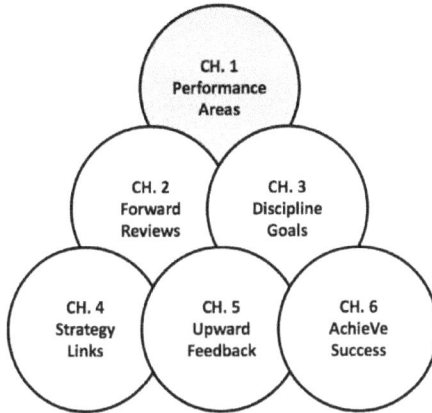

Define behaviors that form career paths for employees,

reinforce core values, and improve critical organizational functions.

Step 1   Select performance areas

Step 2   Identify behavior categories

Step 3   Define experience levels

Step 4   Stretch behaviors across levels

Why Performance Areas?

Who doesn't like going to a nice elegant restaurant for a special occasion? A smiling hostess provides a warm welcome and guides you to a linen-draped table of tall candles, sparkling glasses, and gleaming plates. Gentle music drifts through the air, providing a gentle backdrop to festive conversations. Servers discreetly appear, refilling drinks and delivering exquisitely prepared entrees. Time stands still as you enjoy each mouth-watering bite. You might even indulge in a scrumptious dessert. Best of all, no dishes for you to clean up afterwards!

Now, how would this experience be different if everyone brought their young children? In addition to keeping those tall candles out of reach, you might hear yourself say phrases like "sit up at the table" and "use your indoor voice" mixed in with an occasional curious command like "take that straw out of your nose." Now, we don't mean to say that children and elegant restaurants don't mix. What we are saying is that your role has now changed to include the responsibility of managing their behavior. After all, their idea of a good time in a restaurant may vary greatly from your concept. Your role is to bring alignment to all expectations.

And so it is at work. Our role is to bring alignment to the expectations of individuals from a variety of backgrounds working in a variety of departments within a single organization. A team needs alignment not just in where they are going, but clear expectations as to how they are going to get there. Not unlike the children in the restaurant, we need to ensure that we are explicit in our performance expectations for appropriate behavior (hopefully, there is no need to talk about straws and noses).

Performance expectations are not just about enforcing rules; they are about promoting behaviors that lead to professional and organizational success. These behaviors, informed and guided by these expectations, form the culture of an organization. For performance expectations to become commonly practiced behaviors, they must be explicit, specific, communicated, and measurable.

Most organizations provide job descriptions to define the roles and responsibilities of each position. Job descriptions focus on the specific tasks. We call this the "what" of a job. As important as a job description is towards defining performance, it only provides a partial picture of success for the individual and, ultimately, the organization.

First, job descriptions are limited in the scope of what they can cover. When work functions were simpler and task oriented, job descriptions could detail a comprehensive list of duties an employee would perform. Currently, however, most employees are facing complex situations that don't have a clear "if-then" solution. Customer service employees likely have stated in their job descriptions "to resolve customer complaints," but it can't cover the variety of situations and possible solutions.

Further, as mid-level supervisors have been eliminated, employees are expected to make quick decisions that can carry great impact. With numerous office locations and virtual workplaces, many employees don't work at the same location as the supervisor. Matrix structures have employees collaborating with many individuals within and outside the organization. The fast pace of business requires employees to make rapid decisions with consequences that can travel at the speed of the internet. Employees must not only perform the tasks in their job descriptions, they must also understand and embrace clear performance expectations.

The performance of global organizations can suffer if they have not defined a universal set of performance expectations. Differences in cultural norms can dramatically influence the interactions of employees across borders. A single set of performance areas creates one organizational culture that transcends national cultures. That is not to say that local cultural norms cease to exist. Instead, all employees are given guidance, reinforcement, and encouragement to practice organization-wide behaviors that have been defined for collective success.

Performance expectations aren't something new to employees and supervisors, they usually just haven't been made explicit. Whereas job descriptions

> Fulfilling a job description does not necessarily lead to organizational success.

are the "what" of the position, performance expectations define "how" we go about our work. This is especially true about values. We can heartily agree that we should promote teamwork and ethical conduct, but how do these translate into everyday behaviors? Well-written performance expectations not only reinforce core values, they also highlight core business functions such as customer service, innovation, and new business activities. Performance expectations draw attention to those critical behaviors that employees need to embrace for the organization to remain competitive.

Performance areas also direct individual growth. So often, employees ask what they need to do to get promoted (interestingly, a question asked more and more during onboarding). Performance expectations provide a path for employees to follow to higher skill levels. A clear and explicit set of performance expectations helps employees identify and practice new behaviors that will advance their individual career while improving the performance of the organization.

There are four steps to creating detailed performance areas with explicit behaviors. This chapter will explain how to conduct these steps as summarized below:

Step 1: Select performance areas

Select four to seven performance areas vital to individual and organizational success.

Step 2: Identify behavior categories

Identify specific behaviors that are visible and measurable within each of the selected performance areas.

Step 3: Define experience levels

Determine the skill levels from the entry level positions to the most senior level executives.

Step 4: Stretch behaviors across levels

Describe expectations for specific behaviors across each of the experience levels.

Step 1: Select performance areas

Specific behaviors or expectations are grouped into *performance areas*. The first step in creating a performance management system is to define four core performance areas with up to three optional performance areas. Core performance areas are those expectations that apply to everyone. Examples would be Ethical Conduct, Teamwork, and Job Performance. Optional performance areas are those that apply to large segments of staff, but not everyone. For example, a performance area of Supervisory Skills would only apply to supervisors, and a performance area of Business Development would only apply to those working to develop new opportunities.

Performance areas should reflect the behaviors that the organization most wants to reinforce and assess. The list below is by no means a complete list, but provides some examples of performance areas.

Knowledge & Skills	demonstrating use of the required knowledge and abilities
Job Performance	performing with quality, effectiveness, and timeliness of work
Customer Service	anticipating and fulfilling the needs of clients
Teamwork	collaborating with others toward organizational goals
Ethics	performing work in a way that conforms to accepted standards of conduct
Professional Relationships	representing the organization well to others

Business Development	acquiring new customers and business opportunities
Staff Supervision	attracting, retaining, and developing highly talented employees
Innovation	identifying new products that can be brought to the market
Safety	completing all functions in a manner safe to oneself and others

Again, our task at this stage is to identify four core performance areas; that is, performance areas that will apply to all employees. You can also define up to three optional performance areas that relate to a critical function within your organization and probably applies to a majority or a key segment of your workforce. Feel free to name and define performance areas not in the above list if you don't find ones that speak to your organization. You may even decide to merge similar performance areas.

We are often asked why so few performance areas? Simply put, if everything is a priority, then nothing is a priority. You must decide which performance areas are most critical to the success of your organization. It does not mean that unselected performance areas are not relevant to your organization. They are all important to some degree. Our role as organizational leaders is to define those performance areas that employees can understand and embrace. Too many performance areas run the risk of creating a performance review system that implodes upon itself with the weight of too many expectations.

Step 2: Identify behavior categories

At the risk of overusing an analogy, let's go back to the restaurant. If we said that the restaurant was Italian, we would expect to find certain categories on the menu: pasta, pizza, and wine. At an Indian restaurant, perhaps we would find a tikka, naan, and a lassi. (Can you tell we're writing this chapter too close to dinner time?!) Anyway, once you define the restaurant, you can deduce the categories of dishes. Likewise, now that we have identified the performance area, we can list the categories of behaviors.

For the performance area of **Job Performance**, we could expect behavior categories of:

- time management (managing workload and resources)
- quality (high standards of the final product)
- effectiveness (ability to get the desired results)
- coordination (working seamlessly with other employees).

If we selected the performance area of **Teamwork**, we could unpack it into behavior categories of:

- interaction (positive interpersonal skills)
- participation (involvement in department or organizational activities)
- compliance (adherence to company policies)
- communications (sharing information)
- conflict resolution (resolving differences in a constructive manner).

It is important to breakdown performance areas into behavior categories because we need to eventually define the performance areas in specific and explicit behaviors. It is not enough to say that we expect teamwork from our employees. Nor is it enough to say that we expect participation and compliance. We will need to break these down further into observable behaviors. We'll explain how to do this later in the chapter (in Step 4).

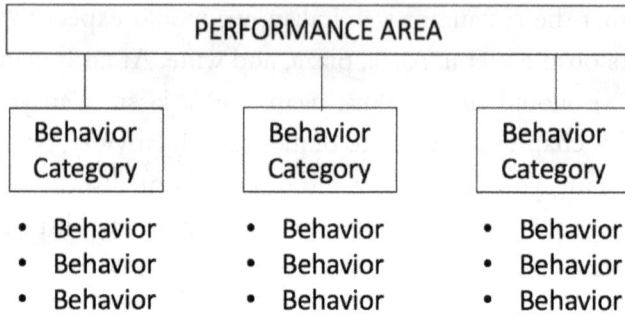

```
┌─────────────────────────────────────────────────┐
│                 PERFORMANCE AREA                 │
└─────────────────────────────────────────────────┘
        │                  │                  │
 ┌────────────┐     ┌────────────┐     ┌────────────┐
 │  Behavior  │     │  Behavior  │     │  Behavior  │
 │  Category  │     │  Category  │     │  Category  │
 └────────────┘     └────────────┘     └────────────┘
   • Behavior         • Behavior         • Behavior
   • Behavior         • Behavior         • Behavior
   • Behavior         • Behavior         • Behavior
```

We have presented these two steps in the order of first identifying performance areas, and then defining the behavior categories. In this deductive method, we start with high level categories and then work our way down into details. We could also use an inductive process by starting with behaviors and then working up into performance areas.

Which method should you use: deductive (top down) or inductive (bottom up)? Well, it depends on what you and your team create when you sit down to make a list of performance areas. If you create a long list of expectations, then you probably have behavior categories that can be grouped into a smaller set of performance areas. If you have a very short list, then these are probably performance areas that need to be defined through further behavior categories.

Whichever method you use, we find it helps teams to list the behavior categories onto cards and to move them into various performance areas until they find a balance and a logic that works for them. It is perfectly fine if there is some overlap between performance areas. We don't need a rigid system with clear boundaries. It is more important to have a listing of performance areas and behavior categories that captures the essence of your organization's expectations.

As you can see, there is no fixed order for these two steps. We can't move past these steps until you have a total of approximately seven performance areas (about four core areas and up to three optional areas). And, each performance area has been detailed further into roughly four to six behavior categories. With this list in hand, you will be ready to move onto the next step of defining levels.

Step 3: Define experience levels

William is a weekend handyman. What does this mean? It means that he has enough skills to take on a home project, but not enough ability to fix everything the first time (or sometimes, the second and third time). If we were to use our lingo from this chapter, we could evaluate William in the 'performance area' of Knowledge & Skills for home repairs.

For example, if you were going to hire someone for a house project, you would have a much higher set of expectations for a professional contractor than you would for William. In other words, you would have different expectations within the performance skill set of plumbing for the professional than you would William. You might expect William to fix a leaky faucet, but you would expect the professional to not only fix the faucet but to replace your water heater, too. They both have skills, but there are levels of expectations that increase with their years of experience and training.

Similarly, we would have different levels of expectations within the performance areas and behavior categories identified in the first two steps. For our example in Step 2, we defined the performance area of Job Performance as having a behavior category of time management. We would have different expectations for an employee's skill in time management based upon her level of experience.

For someone just starting a career, you would have an expectation that she complete tasks in a timely manner. For someone with a few years of experience, you might have an expectation that she can create an accurate timeline in a workplan. And, for someone more senior in your organization, you would expect that she can assign appropriate workloads to employees. These are time management skills, and our expectations increase with the three levels we have defined for these employees.

So, how many levels do we need? In the above example, we had a new employee, mid-level employee, and senior employee. For most organizations, we recommend the following five levels:

- Entry-level
- Junior
- Mid-level
- Senior
- Executive

Few organizations have only five levels or grades. We've seen organizations range from no documented pay grades to as many as seventeen pay grades. Because of this wide variation among organizations, we don't recommend that you determine the number of levels based on the number of pay grades. Instead, we recommend grouping your pay grades into levels, preferably five levels.

We'll use our own organization as an example. Our organization has ten pay grades that range from receptionist clerk in grade one on up to the CEO. We grouped the first two pay grades into entry-level. The next two pay grades became our junior employees. Pay grades five and six became our mid-level employees. Pay grade seven and eight are listed as our senior level employees. And, finally, our pay grades nine and ten are defined as our executive employees.

Let us be clear: There have been no changes to the salaries or benefits of the employees. We have simply grouped them into performance levels. Sometimes we are asked about the need to create groups. In other words, why not simply create an expectation for each pay grade? Because very few, if any, behaviors can be defined into this many levels.

Going back to our time management example, we can expect a clear difference in skills from an employee at pay grade three and an employee at pay grade eight. However, how much difference would we expect between consecutive pay grades, say grades three and four? Surely, we can expect a greater degree of autonomy and quality; but, there isn't necessarily going to be an entirely new skill set. For most behaviors, we have found that five levels allow for an appropriate differentiation in behaviors.

We have described a situation where there are many pay grades, but what if you have few or no pay grades defined? We recommend defining levels for your staff. There are many ways to go about this. The simplest way is to review your organization chart and assign positions to levels based on the similarity of the experience required to perform these positions. You may want to review resources on establishing pay grades or job families. This is important content but outside the purpose of this book.

Step 4: Stretch behaviors across levels

Let's take a quick review of where we are in this process. We defined practice areas (Step 1) and subsets of behavior categories (Step 2). We then defined levels (Step 3). Now we need to 'stretch' the behavior across the levels. We touched on this topic in step three when we gave the time management example across multiple levels. We will take a closer look at this process. To guide us, it is helpful to use a performance area chart. An example is shown on the next page.

In the top row, we have listed Job Performance as the performance area. This is the performance area we have selected as an example. You will create a separate table for each performance area that you have selected. For Job Performance, we have identified four behavior categories: time management, quality, effectiveness, and coordination. These are listed down the left side of the table.

Across the top of the table, we have listed five levels: entry, junior, mid, senior, and executive. In the next row below this, we have listed the pay grades that correspond with the levels. As we explained earlier, multiple pay grades can be aggregated within a single level. This performance area, behaviors, and levels are just an example. You will define the appropriate behaviors and levels for your organization.

We can now fill in the chart by 'stretching' the behavior category across the skill levels. You will see that we have filled in the example behaviors we used earlier for time management. You can see how we have stretched each behavior category across all skill levels in the chart on the next page.

Performance Area: **JOB PERFORMANCE**

Levels → Pay Grades →	Entry 1-2	Junior 3-4	Mid 5-6	Senior 7-8	Executive 9-10
Behavior Categories					
Time management	Completes tasks in a timely manner	Effectively manages own workload	Creates accurate timelines for work plans	Assigns appropriate workloads	Forecasts labor needs to achieve plans
Quality	Completes routine tasks free of mistakes and errors	Conducts work error-free with minimal guidance	Provides recommendations for improving quality	Defines and reinforces quality standards	Sets standards according to industry benchmarks
Effectiveness	Completes assigned work	Makes recommendations to improve department	Ensures that department activities are completed	Ensures that activities are leading to intended results	Defines desired results for departments
Coordination	Communicates task status to supervisor	Collaborates with staff in other departments	Coordinates team responsibilities and use of resources	Ensures department plans are shared with other units	Aligns department expectations with strategic plans

For the entry level of Time Management, we have defined the behavior as "complete tasks in a timely manner." The behaviors grow in complexity as we increase in level. That makes sense, right? Employees at a higher level should demonstrate a greater ability in that specific behavior. Thus, a mid-level employee is expected to "create accurate timelines for workplans." At the senior level, we would see an ability to "forecast labor needs to achieve plans."

These behaviors are cumulative as an employee moves up to higher levels. A mid-level employee is not only expected to create accurate work plans, but should also demonstrate skills in effectively managing her workload and completing tasks in a timely manner. A senior level employee should demonstrate effectiveness in all five behaviors from completing tasks in a timely manner to forecasting labor needs.

Although it is recommended that behaviors at each level be discreetly different from other levels, some overlap is acceptable. Look at the example for the behavior category of quality in the table. The entry level employee is expected to "complete routine tasks free of mistakes or errors" while the junior level employee is expected to "conduct work error-free with minimal guidance." There is some similarity in these expectations. And obviously, no employee goes through a year without making mistakes. However, there is a clear expectation that a supervisor can have a higher level of confidence in the quality of work from a junior level employee than an entry level employee.

Again, our goal is not to create a system with solid boundaries. It is to provide a framework and a path by which employees can assess performance and guide their careers. Don't get caught up in trying to make each level wholly distinct from each level. An employee should be able to see a difference from one level to the next without solid boundaries.

On the performance area chart, we have inserted a row just below the *levels* that shows the *pay grades* for each level. All levels have multiple pay grades. In this chart, the junior level includes pay grades 3 and 4. This is not to say that a grade 3 and a grade 4 are expected to do the same quality of work because they are grouped together. Instead, there should be an expectation that a pay grade 4 will slightly outperform a grade 3 on the same tasks.

Under the behavior category of quality, for example, the junior level is expected to conduct error-free work with minimal guidance. An employee who is pay grade 4 will be expected to produce work at this level and with less guidance more often than a pay grade 3. However, if an employee were promoted to pay grade 5, then he would be expected to provide recommendations for improving quality...but not to the same degree as an employee at pay grade 6 who is also at the same level.

We have listed only one behavior for each of the levels in our example table. However, you should list multiple behaviors within a level. You can list multiple expectations for as many of the skills as you require. There is no limit, but you do want to avoid the table from becoming overly cumbersome. It is better to strive for fewer behaviors than to create a long list.

This chart is for one performance area. You would create a chart for each of your four core performance areas, and a chart for each of the optional performance areas. When you have completed your performance area charts, you will have one page for each one of your performance areas.

One last piece of advice, keep the behaviors simple. Use short phrases, but ensure that behaviors are explicit. Again, overlap is okay from one level to the next, or even across behavior categories and performance areas. Better to have a system that reinforces desired skills than running the risk of omission. Of course, we want you to avoid unnecessary repetition. It is much more important that the listed behaviors are clear, explicit, and simple. They are behaviors that should be observable and measurable.

Congratulations – you have defined your performance areas! This document will become an important tool towards shaping the culture of your organization and the professional development of your employees. It becomes the core component of your entire performance review system.

Additional Thoughts on Performance Areas

After all this work in defining your performance areas, you'll want to be sure that you have an effective roll-out process. You will want to ensure comprehension of the performance areas as well as an understanding of the purpose. As performance areas are one component of the entire performance review process, you may choose to release it along with all changes to the review system that will be described in the upcoming chapters. Or, you may wish to share it now to give employees time to review and comprehend the content. You'll need to decide which way works best for your organization.

If you share the performance areas in advance of an entire system change, be sure to explain that this is intended to provide clear expectations and professional guidance for all employees. We prefer giving employees an opportunity to explore performance related topics in a face-to-face focus group when possible. Giving employees the ability to discuss the content and to ask questions greatly increases the acceptance of a new system.

The number of office locations and overall size of your organization will certainly affect your process for distributing this information. If you have multiple locations, this may mean a phased roll-out or thorough training of regional representatives. Make the document as accessible as possible along with a growing FAQ (frequently asked questions) document of questions asked by employees. And, of course, be sure to include a discussion of the performance areas in your onboarding program for new employees.

In the next chapter, we will explain how to create a Forward Review process using your new performance areas chart.

Action Steps

- ☐ Define performance areas
  (select about four core areas and up to three optional areas)

- ☐ Create list of behavior categories
  (choose four to six behavior categories per performance area)

- ☐ Group pay grades into levels
  (use five levels)

- ☐ Stretch behaviors across levels

Notes & Ideas

Chapter 2: Forward Reviews

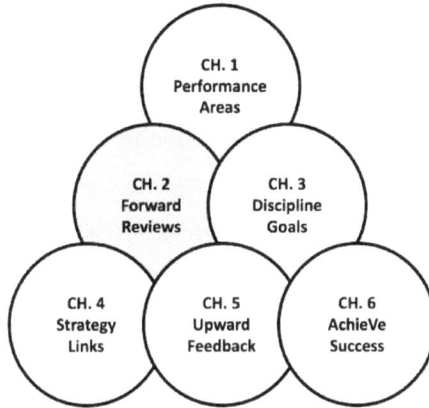

Create a review form that replaces ratings

with meaningful feedback and clear guidance to employees.

Step 1   Create Now+Next boxes

Step 2   Create sentence template

Step 3   Improve self-assessments

Step 4   Establish quality checkpoint

What is a Forward Review?

Imagine that you have traveled to a new city. You get a rental car and head towards your destination for a meeting. The rental car doesn't have a GPS, and your smart phone app can't find this particular street. You are working off a set of driving instructions you wrote down when you first agreed to attend this meeting.

You follow the instructions to the best of your ability. But, after driving by the same landmark you passed a half hour ago, you realize that you are hopelessly lost. At the next stoplight, you roll down your window to call out a question to a friendly-looking person on the sidewalk.

"Where am I?" you ask.

The person calmly replies, "In your car."

You smile politely back, not amused and mindful of the stoplight that will change to green momentarily. You explain the location that you are trying to reach and the directions you are following.

"Oh, yeah, that's far away from here. You really are lost."

By now, the light has turned green and the honking behind you has forced you to continue with the flow of traffic. You are still lost, and that maddening discussion has brought you no closer to your destination.

As silly as this story may sound, many of our performance reviews offer no more guidance than the person on the sidewalk. As a new employee, we are provided the initial expectations and directions given to us, generally in the form of a job description. We then navigate through our weeks and months towards the described destination of good service or successful products.

At the end of the year, we pull over for a short stop to get feedback from our supervisor. We are told some rather obvious expectations about the purpose of our role (that we know already). Perhaps we are told to "keep up the good work" and given some comments about how our work is appreciated.

Our successes are usually given far more attention than our shortcomings. When our achievements are highlighted, the feedback is woefully inadequate. We don't learn about the full impact of our successful actions. Even the phrase 'good job' is frustratingly unhelpful. What made it a good job? What was the impact on the department? What can the employee do to build on this effort to expand skills and help the organization further?

Not that we will remember any of the positive aspects of this conversation. It is the criticism that sticks with us. If we aren't doing well, we are told that we have not arrived at the desired level of performance. We are told that we must work harder to get to our destination. The supervisor encourages the employee to practice new behaviors. Really? As though any of us have ever been successful in truly changing the behavior of another human being. (We've both been married to our spouses for decades; no such luck in changing their behaviors.)

Our performance review meeting abruptly ends, and we merge back into the urgent flow of our work.

Regardless of the nature of the review, the one thing we do remember is our "score." Forget the meaning of the score. The real question we want to ask is "how does this score compare to others?" A score gives us no help with where we are going in our career and how what we do fits in to the bigger picture of the organization. A score is silent on what we should keep doing and what opportunities for growth lie ahead.

As we explained in the introduction, ratings ('3.5 out of 5') and labels ('meets expectations') do not provide nearly enough feedback. Saying 'you are lost' or 'good job' does not help an employee reinforce key behaviors nor leverage these behaviors to achieve new success. We need a *forward review* that helps employees successfully navigate to their destination.

In the previous chapter, we worked on defining performance areas and the specific behaviors expected within each performance area. A forward review provides a clear description of the actions that the employee has taken to arrive at their current location. A forward review then describes the impact of these actions, and how these actions can be adjusted or amplified to achieve future success. After all, the purpose of providing feedback to the employee is not about the past actions and present status, but about defining a clear path to a meaningful destination.

There are four steps to creating a forward review that offers helpful feedback and guidance. This chapter will explain how to conduct these steps as summarized below:

Step 1: Create Now+Next boxes	Establish a format for feedback that informs current and potential performance.
Step 2: Create sentence template	Create a three-part feedback template supervisors can use to deliver meaningful feedback.
Step 3: Improve self-assessments	Emphasize the importance and process by which to communicate a self-evaluation of performance.
Step 4: Establish quality checkpoint	Create a support mechanism to ensure supervisor adoption of the new feedback format.

Step 1: Create Now+Next boxes

Yes, this is the moment you've been waiting for in this book (or dreading). Before we discuss the removal of the rating system, let's be sure we're all talking about the same thing. A rating system is any ranking or rating of employees against a numerical scale or pre-determined categories, such as "below expectations, meets expectations, and exceeds expectations." It is any system where the rating categories have been selected by the company, and it is up to the user to select the appropriate box.

But what will replace them? Short answer: Two empty boxes.

Okay, now for the longer answer. In the previous chapter, we defined performance areas. The form will now have two boxes for each performance area. One box we will call *NOW* and the other box we will call *NEXT*.

NOW	NEXT

In the *NOW* box, the supervisor will write how the employee is demonstrating her skills in this performance area. In the *NEXT* box, the supervisor will describe – specifically – how the employee can enhance her contribution within this performance area in the year ahead. For an example in the performance area of Job Performance, the supervisor could write the following:

Job Performance	
NOW	**NEXT**
Julie demonstrated an ability to submit quality work. She submitted all four quarterly reports on time and without any errors. All statistical information was accurate and narrative provided clear explanations. This resulted in very positive feedback from clients in her region.	Julie should contribute to enhancing quality standards by proposing a list of enhancements to the quarterly report. She should interview clients and collaborate with other staff who write these reports to establish a new set of company standards. This could lead to a company-wide increase of client satisfaction and, ultimately, retention.

In the *NOW* box, the supervisor describes the current performance of the employee. In the *NEXT* box, the supervisor describes the desired future performance of the employee. We'll get into the exact semantics and structure of these statements in the next step. For now, we want to emphasize the simplicity in setting up this section of the review.

For each performance area you established in chapter one, you will list a pair of *Now+Next* boxes. Thus, if you have four performance areas, you'll have four pairs of *Now+Next* boxes. This section of your review form would look like the following page:

Performance Areas

Knowledge & Skills	
NOW	**NEXT**

Job Performance	
NOW	**NEXT**

Professional Relationships	
NOW	**NEXT**

Teamwork	
NOW	**NEXT**

Whether you use an online system or a document-based performance system, be sure that the boxes on your review form can expand easily to accommodate the appropriate amount of narrative.

Although we like the simplicity of *Now* and *Next*, you may choose to replace these with different titles. For example, you could use "Demonstrated Competencies" for *Now* and "Competencies for Development" for *Next* as your headings. Or, you could use "Current Performance" and "Professional Growth" instead. Use whichever terminology fits within your organizational culture. Just be sure that the essence of *Now* and *Next* remains within the descriptions.

Step 2: Create sentence template

If you came upon a friend or co-worker who was collapsed on the floor…what would you do? After calling 911, you could attempt to assist before help arrived. What to do first? Medical experts have created a three-step process of ABC to guide us: Airway, Breathing, and Circulation. With a simple template, people can move forward in an area where they lack expertise or confidence. Writing a performance review isn't nearly as serious, but a template would be just as helpful.

Although not a life-and-death situation, it probably wouldn't surprise you that supervisors might be initially intimidated by the two empty boxes of *Now* and *Next*. Where did the simple check-the-box rating system go? This abrupt change could generate resistance to the new system. We find that people just need more guidance up front until they get comfortable with the new process. They need a template just like the ABC of emergency medical response.

We've found that a feedback sentence is most meaningful when it has three critical components: **specific behavior**, **specific example**, and **specific results**. You might think we are being a bit redundant with the use of the word 'specific' in the last sentence. This is intentional in that we are inundated every day with hollow – that is, nonspecific – feedback.

What is hollow feedback? *I enjoyed your presentation. Great job on the report. You did really well with the client.* These feel good in the moment, but they provide no help in identifying successful behaviors. What was it about the presentation that you enjoyed? What was it about the report that stood out from others? By not having specific feedback, there is no clear path for repeating or enhancing this performance. What was done with this client that could be replicated for others? How do I tell others what I did so that we can all develop better results with our clients? It is important that the feedback be specific, or any benefit from it will quickly disappear.

Specific behavior, specific example, and specific results all contribute to meaningful feedback. This is the structure of the sentences written by the supervisor. Let's review the example feedback from above written in the *Now* box:

NOW
Julie demonstrated an ability to submit quality work. She submitted all four quarterly reports on time and without any errors. All statistical information was accurate and narrative provided clear explanations. This resulted in very positive feedback from clients in her region.

Specific behavior. The first sentence references a specific behavior within the performance area of Job Performance. It is not enough to reference the performance area itself (Job Performance). It is far more meaningful to identify a specific behavior (submit quality work). This can be a behavior listed in the chart, or a behavior that is relevant to the performance area. Whichever you choose, be sure that it is appropriate to the position and experience level.

Specific example. The supervisor continues with specific examples of what made this work high in quality: on time, without any errors, accurate statistical information, and clear narrative. These are all specific examples of the behavior. Listing four quarterly reports shows that this has been consistently achieved.

Specific results. The impact of one's hard work is noted here. Feedback is much more meaningful when we see efforts connected to a desired outcome or organizational goal. In this example, the quarterly reports led to higher satisfaction by clients. Any specific, tangible, and measurable results are helpful in showing the results. It shows that the work is meaningful, appreciated, and worthy of further development.

This leads us to the *NEXT* box. In this box, we follow the exact same format of specific behavior, specific example, and specific results. The verb tense changes from the past to the future, but the structure remains intact. Let's look at the feedback written in the *NEXT* box:

NEXT
Julie should contribute to enhancing quality standards by proposing a list of improvements to the quarterly report. She should interview clients and collaborate with other staff who write these reports to establish a new set of company standards. This could lead to a company-wide increase of client satisfaction and, ultimately, retention.

Specific behavior. The first sentence describes the specific behavior of "enhancing quality standards by proposing a list of improvements." This behavior is listed in the performance area of Job Performance. It appropriately builds on the past performance of the employee in providing quality work. Instead of merely submitting quality work, she will be enhancing quality standards.

Specific example. The specific example is to "propose a list of enhancements to the quarterly report." The feedback includes a proposed course of action for interviewing clients and collaborating with other staff. This may not be the only way in which she can enhance quality standards, but it provides a clear example to build on.

Specific results. The specific result is a "company-wide increase of client satisfaction and retention." This specific impact provides a clear incentive for the company, supervisor, and employee to invest in this development activity. It sets a clear path for the continued growth of the employee by further developing her ability to deliver quality within the organization.

By giving supervisors a sentence template, you will help them to adopt this new format for writing reviews.

- *NOW* sentence template

  The employee has demonstrated an ability to…(specific behavior)…by doing…(specific examples)…which has resulted in…(specific results).

- *NEXT* sentence template

  The employee should demonstrate an ability to…(specific behavior)…by doing…(specific examples)…which would result in…(specific results).

So far we have been discussing how to reinforce good performance. How do we address the issue of poor performance?

You might be wondering if this format works for poor performance. As we explained above, the purpose of an AchieVe review is to build on the talents and abilities of individuals towards organizational goals. There are times when a poor performance hinders the ability of an employee to be successful. In these cases, the *Now+Next* format and the specific sentence structure provide clear corrective guidance to these employees.

Using a variation of the above example, we could see the following statements for an employee struggling to perform at expected quality performance standards:

Quality	
NOW	**NEXT**
Pat has not demonstrated an ability to submit quality work consistently. Of the four quarterly reports, three were submitted late. Statistical errors were found in all four reports. This contributed to a lowering of client satisfaction in her region.	Pat should consistently produce quality work as expected for her position. This includes submitting quarterly reports on time and without errors. This will contribute to a higher satisfaction and retention rate of clients within the region.

In the *NOW* box, we have identified the specific behavior (produce quality work consistently), specific example (quarterly reports late and with errors), and specific results (lower client satisfaction). Likewise, the *NEXT* box shows the specific behavior (consistently produce quality work), specific example (quarterly reports on time and without errors), and specific results (higher satisfaction rate of clients).

At times, there may be a mismatch of skills or fit between an individual and the requirements of the position. We can identify the skill set and use this feedback format to align the identified skills with the desired outcomes of the position or department. Using this format, we can articulate the specific behaviors that do exist and identify the specific examples and potential results that could be realized with these behaviors. Rarely is a mismatch irreparable. This format helps supervisors find a path for employees to contribute their skills in a way that results in meaningful outcomes.

The imaginary reviews above are just that, imagined. For actual reviews, we would encourage more narrative on the description of specific examples. But not much more. In the example reviews above, there would likely be additional examples of quality achieved (or not achieved) by the employee. A few more examples would be warranted to show that the desired (or undesired) behavior is in fact a consistent behavior and not a one-off exception. The purpose is to document examples and not to narrate an entire year's worth of activities. You will only need a few examples to properly illustrate a behavior.

Step 3: Improve self-assessments

When you go to the doctor's office, what happens before you see the doctor? Okay, other than flipping through old magazines. You complete a medical self-assessment form. On this form, you describe existing allergies, past surgeries, current symptoms, exercise habits, and other necessary information. With this document, the doctor can give you sound feedback and guidance. So it is with the performance review (without the stale magazines).

When individuals talk to us about the performance review form, they primarily focus on how the supervisor uses the form. We shift the conversation to how the employee uses the form, which is critical to generate meaningful feedback from the supervisor. Just as you wouldn't go into a medical exam and have the doctor guess your conditions, employees shouldn't go into a performance review and expect supervisors to discern a year's worth of activity without the employee's self-assessment.

There is another reason we emphasize self-assessment. Who's ultimately responsible for the employee's career? The supervisor? Human resources? Do any of us really want to put our career into the hands of anyone else? No. It is our own responsibility to shape our own careers.

There's also a sad but true reality that few of us will be lucky enough to have attentive supervisors throughout our entire career. I'm sure you can look back on your career and note times when you had supervisors who were not as engaged about your career development as you would have liked. Especially as organizations streamline operations, there will be more employees reporting to a single person or working in a matrixed organization with multiple supervisors. Employees empowered with the ability to conduct self-assessments will still grow and develop during these periods in their career.

In this chapter, we will shift emphasis to the employee's self-assessment. Many organizations already have a self-assessment component that the employee submits to the supervisor. Often, it is a self-promotional marketing piece: Look at how awesome I was this year! The motivation is receiving a high score, not to spark a meaningful conversation about an employee's future. Is there sincere reflection on behalf of the employee? What learning has been acquired, and how has this been applied? Has the employee identified a direction for professional growth? These are elements of a truly introspective and meaningful self-assessment.

The employee can use the same sentence template in constructing a self-assessment. For each performance area, the employee writes a *Now* and *Next* statement with the three elements of specific behavior, specific examples, and specific results. Here's an example from the Teamwork performance area:

Teamwork	
NOW	**NEXT**
I have demonstrated an ability to collaborate with colleagues by participating on a process improvement team. Our team generated new policies that reduced procurement costs by 17 percent.	I can continue improving my ability to collaborate with colleagues by engaging new employees to serve on our process improvement teams. Bringing in people with recent experience at other organizations could provide new perspectives that generate new ideas and create additional savings for our company.

This *NOW* example reveals the three elements of a complete performance evaluation: specific behavior (collaborate with colleagues), specific example (participating on a process improvement team), and specific results (new policies that reduced costs by 17 percent). The *NEXT* statement shows growth in a specific behavior (collaborate with colleagues) with a specific example (engaging new employees to serve on a process improvement team) and a specific result (generate new ideas and additional savings).

A thorough self-assessment provides a solid foundation for the supervisor to write the review. The supervisor can focus energy on reading the self-assessment and providing guidance to the employee based on the supervisor's perspective.

This is more helpful and practical. Think about the last 12 months. Can you recall everything that your direct reports accomplished? Particularly for those of us who can't recall what we had for lunch yesterday, remembering the activities of employees during the last year would be challenging.

Further, a thorough self-assessment can help a supervisor avoid 'recency bias' when writing a review. Recency bias occurs when we draw a conclusion, good or bad, based on the most recent memories we have about a topic. A supervisor could be tempted to recall events that happened in the last 60 days, but not consider events that occurred at the beginning of the year. A well-documented self-assessment will help supervisors avoid the recency bias.

For these reasons, the self-assessment is very important. In fact, we encourage spending twice as much time on training employees for self-assessments versus time spent with supervisors about the performance review process. This self-assessment training includes monthly journaling, skill mapping, and other actions that employees can do to inform feedback and shape performance. This empowers employees to be responsible for their careers. Further, it empowers supervisors to focus on guidance and support, and not on recollection and recordkeeping.

Step 4: Establish quality checkpoint

Let's be honest. Giving someone a rating is easy. Writing a *Now+Next* statement requires a bit more practice. It is crucial to have a quality control step in the process, particularly when first launching this new review process. Supervisors will benefit when employees are providing insightful self-assessments. They will also benefit from having a sentence template to craft better feedback sentences. Further, a quality control point ensures that the supervisor is communicating an accurate and appropriate message to the employee. Your quality control checkpoint needs to provide three elements: confidentiality, coaching, and collaboration.

> *Confidentiality.* It goes without saying (but we'll say it anyway) that performance reviews are dealing with matters that are both personal and confidential. It's important that the person who is reviewing the *Now+Next* statements can do so without betraying the confidentiality of the employee or the supervisor. It is rather obvious that we need to protect the confidentiality of the employee. However, we also want to be sure that the supervisor can feel safe in providing less-than-perfect statements for feedback without feeling threatened. With a safe dialogue, the quality checkpoint can also contribute to the next element of coaching.

> *Coaching.* As much as we can define the science behind the sentence structure, there is likewise an art to crafting meaningful feedback. Whether supervisor and employee have similar or different styles, it is important to balance the tone of the feedback statements to clearly communicate a message. Providing an independent perspective can go a long way in helping a supervisor improve on the writing of these critical feedback sentences. Ensuring that these sentences are written clearly, with examples, and with a way forward leads to the final element of quality control: collaboration.

Collaboration. The purpose of the performance management system is to find a collaborative way forward that aligns the priorities of the employee with the objectives of the organization. The feedback sentences must reflect this collaboration. These sentences provide the foundation of the dialogue and plans moving forward. Whether the sentences are leaning towards praise or towards correction, they need to be framed in a spirit of collaboration that moves the dialogue and relationship forward. The quality checkpoint can help to ensure this collaboration.

In this step, you'll need to identify a checkpoint. We suggest that these *Now+Next* statements are sent by the supervisor to the checkpoint for review. The checkpoint should be someone who can offer the confidentiality, coaching, and collaboration described above. Quite often, human resources is a checkpoint. However, this may not always be possible, especially in larger organizations. You may also consider identifying key upper level managers to act as quality control for the reviews within their span of control. This may make some supervisors nervous to present their imperfect sentences to upper management. It is a trade-off that you will need to consider.

Wherever you place your quality checkpoint, you'll need to ensure two additional pieces are in place: capacity and commitment. To ensure capacity, appropriate training and guidance is given to the individuals providing quality control. These individuals should practice writing *Now+Next* statements and to provide feedback to each other in small groups. This will help the quality control people come to a common understanding of how they will collectively monitor this process in a consistent manner.

The second piece, commitment, is to ensure that those in the role of providing feedback will do so in an agreed amount of time. This is often a challenge with the daily workload and newly emerging issues in an organization. Those serving as quality control checkpoints must commit to providing this turnaround. Otherwise, it can become a frustration for supervisors and a bottleneck in the process. Likewise, you don't want to enforce the time turnaround so emphatically that quality reviewing becomes a perfunctory activity ('Yeah, sure, looks good to me.'). So, find a reasonable time for the checkpoint turnaround and communicate this expectation widely across the organization.

Additional Thoughts on Forward Reviews

In the entire AchieVe system, this is likely to be the most challenging chapter to complete. Getting rid of ratings is not easy. In a world that seeks to count the number of likes on social media and get the highest scores on everything from Uber to Yelp, we are almost lost without a rating. However, as we explained in the introduction, ratings provide no meaningful information to employees and can even distract from helpful feedback.

Every organization is different. If your organization is immediately open to throwing out the ratings (or has already done so), then you are well on your way. The rest of this book will guide you in the process of strengthening your performance management system.

If, however, your organization is resistant to eliminating ratings, then you'll need to consider your next course of action. You can pause and work to change the minds, attitudes, and culture of the organization. In general, we suggest that this will not likely lead to the change you desire. Culture tends to follow practice; culture tends to entrench against attacks.

So, what then? We suggest that you build and pilot. You can finish the book and build the system. If you are successful in changing minds, then the system is ready to go. Or, build the system and seek a department or division that can pilot the new approach. Collect this feedback and continue the dialogue with decision makers.

Action Steps

☐ Create *Now+Next* boxes
(choose wording the reflects your organization's culture)

☐ Create sentence template
(build on the three elements of specific behavior, specific example, and specific result)

☐ Improve self-assessments
(use the *Now+Next* format)

☐ Establish quality checkpoint
(ensure capacity and commitment)

Notes & Ideas

Chapter 3: Discipline Goals

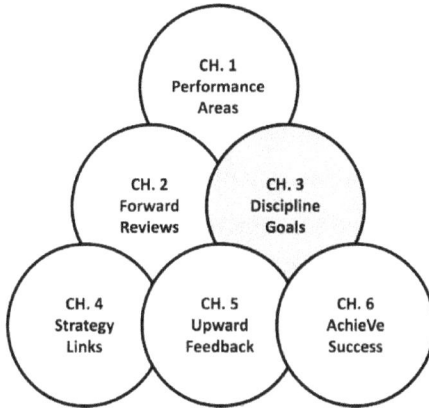

Define discipline goals that provide a foundation for

job performance, career advancement, and deeper purpose.

.

Step 1	Determine discipline goals
Step 2	Provide a measure
Step 3	Ask for less
Step 4	Evaluate past goals

What is a discipline?

There are jobs. There are careers. And then there are disciplines.

A job gives you a paycheck. A career provides a deeper contribution to a specific field. A discipline defines purpose and strives for mastery. You can get a job. You can have a successful career (or two). A discipline, however, is never truly achieved. That is not to say that someone who pursues a discipline is not able to demonstrate considerable skill. Quite the opposite! However, within a discipline, the pursuit never stops. Pursuing a discipline is to forever strive for higher levels of comprehension and creation.

Therefore, when we use the word *discipline* we are not speaking about someone having the discipline to avoid sugary foods or having the discipline to get up and run every morning. Instead, we use the word to say that someone is pursuing a discipline such as playing an instrument or writing fiction. We do not only seek a mere list of actions; we also seek purpose and mastery.

Along the spectrum from job to career to discipline, the performance review focuses on the discipline through the selection of discipline goals. Helping employees to define and articulate the discipline in which they want to develop provides a foundation on which the career and the job are built. Without a clear sense of discipline, a job is just a job and a career can become as hollow as a mere series of jobs. A discipline goal gives meaning within a job and an opportunity to pursue mastery throughout the career.

The job and career are very important. The job description describes the specific elements of the position as part of the hiring agreement. The resume demonstrates a proven record of achievement and professional growth. The performance review is the opportunity to define the discipline goal, and to link the goal to the functions of the position.

Simply naming the discipline goal is not enough. A goal must have a clear measure for two reasons: direction and distance. A discipline goal's purpose is to seek improvement, but it is a very broad and deep category of knowledge and skill. A measure provides an explanation as to the forward progress a person is taking within that discipline.

For example, if someone wanted to develop the discipline of public speaking, the measures of "audience satisfaction score" and "number of new topics" define different directions. The measure of *audience satisfaction score* indicates a focus on continually refining and sharpening a specific approach or presentation. The *number of new topics* pushes towards developing a public speaking portfolio of many topics. Both measures indicate a deepening of one's ability in the discipline of public speaking, but in different directions.

The second reason for a having a clear measure is distance. How far has a person gone in the pursuit of a discipline? A measure will answer that question. For the measures offered above as an example for public speaking, an increase in the *audience satisfaction score* will certainly indicate our progress. Also, the *number of new topics* measure will show if we are expanding our portfolio at the pace we anticipated.

Within a discipline goal, measures define the direction of progress and assess the distance achieved. Measures play one other vital role in today's rapidly changing world: flexibility.

Change is a constant. As organizations change to adapt to new market opportunities or external conditions, so must the individuals within these organizations change. Does that mean that when the organization makes a significant change, the individual must change their goals? No, not if the employee has a discipline goal.

A discipline goal is broad enough to cover assignments, jobs, and even careers. The measure can be adapted to the changing needs of the department and organization. In this manner, a measure offers flexibility to the individual in shaping the direction and distance within the discipline goal. If the particular measure chosen is not accomplished due to changing circumstances, the progress toward the discipline goal can still be captured through a different measure. The discipline goal, however, remains untouched and serves as a constant focus for an employee in an ever-changing world.

There are four steps to discipline goals that provide focus and growth for employees. This chapter will explain how to conduct these steps as summarized below:

Step 1: Determine discipline goals | Guide employees to find the deeper intent and purpose within their choice of job and career.

Step 2: Provide a measure | Select measures to indicate annual progress towards gaining mastery within each discipline.

Step 3: Ask for less | Reconcile ambitions with realistic expectations as to what can be achieved in a year.

Step 4: Evaluate past goals | Examine prior goals to better understand individual achievement and external factors.

Step 1: Determine discipline goals

One of the best methods to ensure that we do something that takes time and attention is to set a goal. Goals have been a fixture within performance evaluations for as long as performance evaluations have existed. We have observed that most goals in evaluations are little more than task lists. There is nothing wrong with helping employees focus on what needs to be accomplished; but if we want our evaluations to be a development tool for employees and ensure organizational objectives are fulfilled, we need to elevate use of goal-setting to something that can help employees develop professionally.

Meaningful goals need to reflect a discipline. Disciplines are not only for talented musicians and skilled doctors. Every person in every position can define a discipline goal. But how to go about this? How does one determine a discipline? We have found five critical questions to ask: Why? Why? Why? Why? and Why?

No, that's not a mistake. We are asking the *Why?* question multiple times. By doing this, the *Why?* question becomes a shovel to help us dig down several layers to get to the foundation of an employee's ambition. When we interview employees about their goals at work, they typically define either tasks (for the job) or growing into a new position (for the career). We want to use our shovel question (Why?) to dig deeper to get to the discipline.

At one of our workshops, we asked participants to share their goals from their last performance review. One person stated that they wanted to attend an intensive two-week supervisor training program. We started digging with our shovel question:

Why do you want to attend the intensive two-week supervisor training program?

Because I want to learn supervising skills.

Why?

Because I want my staff to be happy.

Why?

Because I want to retain employees I manage.

Why?

Because I want to increase the performance of the department.

Why?

Because I want to be able to lead a successful team.

There we go. Now our shovel starts to hit something hard at the bottom of all that digging. This last answer begins to define the discipline goal. Attending a training is a task, not a discipline goal. Learning about supervising is (hopefully) a result of the task. The next two items speak to department performance that lead to a (hopeful) result of achieving the organization's goals. Underneath all of this, we find the discipline. Now we are ready to select a discipline goal.

Typically, we can tell if a discipline goal is in fact stated as a true discipline goal when it completes the following sentence: *I will improve my ability to…*(insert sentence). For example, *"I will improve my ability to attend a two-week supervisor training program"* doesn't sound like much of an aspiration. Neither does *"I will improve my ability to retain employees I manage."* This is an important activity to pursue, but it does not speak to deeper purpose nor give a description of the method.

Using the last answer in the five "whys" exercise *"I will improve my ability to lead a successful team"* is a discipline goal that builds a solid foundation for the job. It is a goal that can transcend a career and even carry over to multiple careers. This is a goal that goes beyond the day-to-day tasks to resonate with the individual.

The answers to these shovel questions will and do vary. There are many different paths that the questions could follow. In the example shown above, we have many participants who all start from a similar initial goal of attending a skills training but have diverged into a wide-array of disciplines that each resonated with the individual:

- *I will improve my ability to coach and develop employees*
- *I will improve my ability to contribute to organizational success*
- *I will improve my ability to develop tomorrow's leaders*
- *I will improve my ability to develop trusted relationships with clients*
- *I will improve my ability to develop new business*

Once you begin digging with the shovel question, there's no telling where you will end up. Well, other than deeper. To say, "*I will improve my ability to attend a training*" or "*I will improve my ability to supervise*" suddenly sounds uninspiring. To say, instead, "*I will improve my ability to lead a successful team*" defines a discipline goal that one can develop.

Every employee can have a discipline goal. The newest employee in the most junior position can have a discipline goal. Many organizations have an office clerk as an entry level position. This position ensures that many of the behind-the-scenes functions are completed and necessary resources are made available to all staff. If so, then a discipline goal could be to "improve my ability to create a positive work environment." There are many other possible discipline goals for this position. Every person, regardless of position, can – and should – have a discipline goal.

Ask employees to list potential discipline goals to pursue. These are goals that should resonate with them, and that they feel would be relevant for many years. Assure people if the goals don't jump out immediately. It takes time to reflect and consider possible discipline statements. Writing tasks is easy. Reflecting on the deeper purpose takes more effort. Keep using the shovel question to help people dig deeper and reach the foundation of their tasks and activities.

DISCIPLINE GOAL
I will improve my ability to…

Step 2: Provide a measure

We're not fans of the whole push for SMART goals. Are they dead yet? We hope so. They are over-stated and not very useful in implementation. Often, when we counsel supervisors on goals they immediately say "Oh, yeah, I know, we have to use SMART goals." When we ask for a definition of a SMART goal, they usually can't recall the elements of the acronym. Go ahead and give it a try. Can you name the parts of the acronym?

How did you do?

It gets better. If we ask a room full of supervisors, there is a wide variation. The S has stood for strategic, specific, significant, stretching, and sustainable. For the M we've heard measurable, meaningful, and motivational. The A has included attainable, achievable, accepted, action-oriented and so on. A tool, even a simple mnemonic device, isn't helpful if people can't use it.

So, no SMART goals here.

When we look at a discipline goal, the most important element we've found is that individuals need to know the progress that they are making along the path of their discipline. Although they will likely never reach the end of this path ("Ta-da, I know all there ever is to know about leading employees"), people do need a way to measure distance achieved.

Thus, a discipline goal requires a measure.

A measure is how you will measure progress deeper into the discipline. Since most performance reviews are written on an annual cycle, the measure should focus on the amount of progress achieved in that year. For a discipline goal, a measure indicates the milestone that the individual can expect to achieve in a specific amount of time.

Let's use a goal from earlier in this chapter as an example: *"I will improve my ability to lead a successful team."* Possible measures could be:

- Cross-training all tasks in the department is achieved
- Quarterly development sessions with each employee are conducted
- Turnover in the department is reduced
- Department objectives are met

There are many measures that can be selected. What guidelines to use when selecting a measure? A measure is primarily defined by two factors: the skill level of the individual and the current need of the organization.

It is critical to ensure that the measure matches the skill level of the individual. A measure that is too easy will not inspire growth. On the flip side, a measure that is too difficult can diminish an employee's self-confidence.

The second factor is the current need of the organization. The individual striving to be a stellar supervisor may want to promote all of his employees, but do these measures fit within the needs of the organization? Will these measures achieve a specific organizational strategy? An effective measure considers both the skill level of the employee and the needs of the organization.

A discipline goal (*I will improve my ability to lead a successful team*) can stay the same for years, even a lifetime. The measure, however, can and should change annually to reflect career growth and new organizational needs. The discipline goal defines the purpose; the measure defines the progress.

One of the common questions we get about setting goals is "What if something changes during the year that makes my goals irrelevant or impossible to do?" With a discipline goal, we don't see that happening unless you are making a serious career overhaul. Midyear, are you really going to stop striving to be a better supervisor?

Sometimes, however, an organizational change occurs that will affect a goal. Let's look at this example:

- Discipline goal: *Improve my ability to improve operational efficiency.*
- Measure: *Staff conversion to a new software is complete by year end.*

However, the organization decides to delay the conversion of the software product. Does that mean that the goal is to be thrown out? No, just change the measure. Let's look again at the example:

- Discipline goal: *Improve my ability to improve operational efficiency.*
- Measure: *All team members are prepared for software conversion.*

The goal has remained the same. The measure has been adapted to the new situation. The actions described in the measure will not only help the organization now but will lead to better implementation of future software conversions, once they are finally approved.

Ask employees to define a few measures for each discipline goal. These measures will be reviewed and refined in the next step.

Discipline Goal	**Measures**
I will improve my ability to…	

Step 3: Ask for less

When people start talking about discipline goals, deeper intentions, and meaningful measures…they get excited. And when they get excited, they can get a little carried away. Most often, people will define numerous disciplines and several measures for each discipline. This is good. We like excitement!

But, realistically, how many goals can one person truly pursue well? Think about your personal life. With all the demands on your time, how many new hobbies can you explore, how many new sports can you play, and how many subject matters can you study? If we're lucky, one. Maybe, just maybe, two. So it is for work.

What? Just two discipline goals? Yes, two are plenty. These are disciplines, not tasks. There could be hundreds of tasks related to a single discipline. You can complete a hundred tasks. But how many different discipline goals can a person actively pursue over a year's time? In your personal life, could you become a pianist, complete marathon training, learn a new language, and acquire fancy cooking skills? Not likely. Yet, how tempted are we to list multiple items on our professional goals. These are the essential elements of your career and performance. Most people can handle two of these. One is fine, three is pushing it.

Ask employees to review their disciplines goals and select two. These two should most represent their career projection and the needs of the organization. There is a possibility that two closely related goals could be merged together. However, avoid creating a long run-on sentence that is really two separate goals linked with an 'and' in the middle.

For example, the two goals "improve my ability to lead a successful team" and "improve my ability to lead marketing campaigns" could be combined into "improve my ability to lead successful marketing campaign teams." However, the goal of "improve my ability to develop new products" and "improve my ability to provide leadership in financial decision-making" should probably be kept separate.

How many measures? Let's review the purpose of a measure. A measure helps us to determine our progress along the discipline path. Measures also gives us flexibility. In Step 2 we explained that if there is a change in the organizational environment, then the measures can be changed to reflect the new reality.

The broad definition of a discipline goal conceivably provides an endless number of potential measures. With only one measure, the employee might be limited if there are limited opportunities afforded by the organization to pursue that exact measure. If an employee has too many measures, then it will be difficult for the employee to focus energy around a specific component of the goal. Three measures for each goal often strikes a balance between flexibility and focus.

Now, ask employees to look at the number of measures they've selected for each goal. Ask them to adjust the number of measures to about three for each goal. Congratulations, your team now has defined discipline goals!

Career Trajectory

Organizational Needs

Discipline Goals

Step 4: Evaluate past goals

When we discuss professional goals with individuals, we ask them: Can you tell me your explicit goals for this year? Most people cannot do so. In our workshops, we ask people to raise their hands if they wrote goals for this year. Nearly everyone has a hand in the air. We then ask which people could recite their goals right now. Only a couple of hands remain in the air.

It is as if pursuing goals is a one-time exercise to be done with the annual performance review. They are written down and promptly forgotten for a year, until it is time to write a new set of goals. Often, the goals were completed because they were nothing more than a list of tasks that the employee was going to work on as part of their job responsibilities. Or, worse, nothing at all happened.

We can all do a lot to act upon our meaningful goals during the year. At a minimum, we need to ensure that staff evaluate their goals from the prior year before writing new goals. If the goals are discipline goals, the employee will be able to assess their progression within their chosen profession. They should ask themselves these three questions:

How did I progress toward my measures? This question should have a purely evaluative and empirical answer. This is where it is critical that a measure was created alongside the goal. If you have just converted to discipline goals with clear measures, employees may not have measures by which to assess previous goals. Instead, ask employees to document specific examples of progress made towards the goal.

Remember, if the goal were a true discipline goal, then the employee will likely never fully master it. The employee should have made clear progress towards that goal by achieving some milestones, accomplishments, or measures that represent the discipline goal. At some point, an employee may reach a level of mastery that is sufficient and choose to focus on some other aspect of their profession.

What new behaviors did I adopt to progress towards this goal? How the employee has consciously and systematically altered performance reflects the level of mastery of this discipline goal. This helps the employee to identify and acknowledge the effort towards this goal. This also helps to show that progress was not attained by the mere existence of this measure. New and sustained effort was required. A sales measurement may have been reached purely due to external factors that had little or nothing to do with an individual's efforts. Likewise, reaching a specific measure may not have been possible even with a host of new behaviors due to an overwhelming external condition. This leads us to the next question.

What external factors influenced my discipline goal? As indicated in the above question, there are situations when external factors help or hinder our progress towards a discipline goal. This is where some people will seek to throw out the goal altogether. This is a critical reason for distinguishing between a discipline goal and a measure. A well-crafted and thoughtful discipline goal will weather nearly all changes that can come about in a year. The goal remains; it is the measure that changes.

In this last question, the employee can reflect on the external influences that impacted this discipline goal. Perhaps the external influences made the measure easy to attain. In this case, what did the employee do to attain a higher or more difficult measure? Or, perhaps external factors made the measure difficult or even irrelevant to attain. In which case, how did the employee select a different measure that demonstrates growth within the discipline? What steps did the employee take towards attaining this measure?

By answering these three questions, the employee can learn from the efforts of the last year towards the old goals. With this reflection, the employee can look ahead to shaping critical discipline goals for the year with relevant and reasonable measures to reflect progress towards the discipline.

Ask employees to answer the three questions above. Even if they have recently defined the discipline goal, it is highly likely that they have already been working towards this goal. They may have not explicitly defined it and identified measures; however, they have likely been working within this discipline. Ask them to reflect on the questions and write their responses.

After writing their responses, ask them to review their measures. Will the selected measures provide a clear assessment of progress in the discipline? Is it evident as to the behaviors that will be needed to achieve these measures? Is there enough flexibility across the measures to overcome the most likely external factors? The employees should adjust their measures, if needed, to address these questions.

PREVIOUS GOALS	
Goal	**Measures**
How did I progress toward my measures?	
What new behaviors did I adopt?	
What external factors influenced my ability to reach this goal?	

Additional Thoughts on Discipline Goals

Writing a discipline goal will likely be the most difficult task for employees when completing a self-review. Conceptually, a discipline goal resonates well with most individuals. The act of writing a discipline goal; however, is a bit more difficult for individuals to grasp.

Like any new skill, writing a discipline goal takes practice. Remind people to use the "Improve my ability to…" structure to ensure that their goal is not merely a task. Self-reflection is necessary at this stage. Asking the question "why" repeatedly is helpful. We have observed that people find talking it out with a trusted colleague to be helpful in articulating the discipline.

Once people have identified a goal, encourage them to identify several measures that reflect the direction and distance that they anticipate achieving in this discipline. When introducing this concept, you could consider encouraging teams to share their goals and measures to facilitate learning.

In chapter six we will discuss quality controls for the entire review process. Discipline goals are a critical component to be monitored through the quality control process. Until people get in the habit of writing discipline goals, you'll need to ensure that someone is coaching and helping them define their disciplines appropriately.

Finally, be sure to push back on too many goals. Some individuals and organizations create a mindset that more is better. That is not true in this case. A discipline goal requires focus, and a consistent amount of sustained energy over a long period of time. Stay firm in making people choose the top two discipline goals that they will pursue.

Action Steps

☐ Write examples of discipline goals
(choose examples relevant to your organization)

☐ For each discipline goal example, write illustrative measures
(write measures for each grade level)

☐ Set an appropriate limit on the number of discipline goals for individuals in your organization

☐ Define reflection questions for past goals
(modify the three questions from this chapter)

Notes & Ideas

Chapter 4: Strategy Links

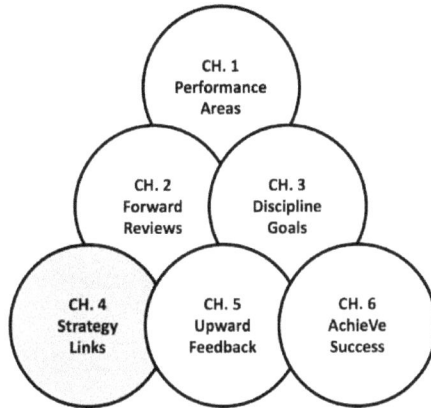

Establish a process that empowers employees

to link individual goals to organizational objectives.

Step 1	Create a strategy map
Step 2	Disseminate strategy map
Step 3	Link goals to strategies
Step 4	Aggregate links

Why do we need a strategy map?

There are two great stories about the importance of linking the mission to individual performance. One involves a janitor and the other a stone-cutter.

As the popular story goes, on May 25, 1961, President Kennedy announced the ambition of sending a man to the moon and safely returning him to earth. Various organizations had to operationalize this vision, including NASA. Soon after the speech, President Kennedy visited NASA to inspire and communicate with the teams that would be making this vision a reality.

President Kennedy met hundreds of employees and asked about the work that they did. During his visit, he encountered a janitor sweeping the floor. As with other employees, he asked the janitor what he did at NASA, to which the janitor replied, "I am helping to put a man on the moon."

Likewise, there is the stone-cutter legend. Christopher Wren, an accomplished English architect, decided to walk the grounds – incognito – to see firsthand the progress on building St. Paul's cathedral in London. Walking past the stonecutters, he asked each what they were doing. The first one replied, "I am cutting a piece of stone for the side wall." The second replied, "I am earning five shillings per day."

Christopher Wren continued this type of inquiry with the various workers when he came upon a third stonecutter who replied, "I am helping Sir Christopher Wren build a beautiful cathedral for England."

Both examples illustrate how an employee can link their individual efforts to the compelling mission of the organization. Ultimately, an organization can only be successful if individuals are successful in their individual tasks and if those individual tasks are aligned with the objectives of the organization.

We might be tempted to think that it is the role of management to align individual efforts to the common goals. Yes, to an extent. We also recognize that our flatter, leaner organizations of today must have a fast and responsive workforce that can quickly adapt and implement successful activities. Employees who understand their role and the link to organizational objectives will be able to make these adjustments more quickly.

Let's step back just a moment to the higher intention motivating all human beings: We want to contribute to something meaningful. Unfortunately, how many employees identify with the stonecutter who defined what he did as earning five shillings a day? How much more successful would organizations be, if we could tap into the desire to contribute that resides in all our employees?

Organizations strive to enhance benefits, provide raises, issue promotions, give recognition, and develop staff skills. These are all important endeavors. However, a foundation beneath these efforts is the motivation to contribute to something meaningful. An organization that establishes a process for helping employees link their individual discipline goals to larger objectives – and the mission of the organization – will have a motivated and adaptable workforce.

To facilitate these connections between an individual discipline goal and an organizational objective, we need a strategy map. Just as the name indicates, a strategy map provides a simple visual layout of the primary objectives of the organization. This strategy map distills the strategic plans of the organization into clear and compelling language.

Most organizations don't have a single clear purpose like putting a man on the moon or building a cathedral. Organizations often have a complex compilation of various strategies, priorities, and objectives that need to be achieved. The strategy map distills all this information into a single diagram.

Depending on the organization, creating the strategy map might involve translating jargon-speak into clear objectives. Or, it might include breaking down vague intentions into specific objectives. The strategic objectives of the organization are simplified and communicated through the strategy map.

With a completed strategy map, employees can link their individual goals to the organizational objectives. These strategy links can be aggregated across departments and divisions to identify opportunities for further support and encouragement. Knowing who is working on which organizational objectives will help allocate resources towards the appropriate activities.

There are four steps to creating strategy links between individual discipline goals and organizational objectives. This chapter will explain how to conduct these steps as summarized below:

Step 1: Create a strategy map — Summarize primary organizational objectives into a visual reference resource for employees.

Step 2: Disseminate strategy map — Share strategy map with employees and ensure understanding of the organizational objectives.

Step 3: Link goals to objectives — Guide employees in linking individual discipline goals with organizational objectives.

Step 4: Aggregate links — Aggregate individual links to organizational objectives to support and coordinate efforts.

Step 1: Create a strategy map

Organizations typically have no shortage of strategies and goals. They are often communicated in some type of table or chart. They are often some combination of objectives, strategies, goals, tasks, actions, and priorities. Our goal is to simplify what the organization is trying to accomplish into a simple and readable visual diagram.

We don't propose one single way in which all organizations should categorize their various initiatives. We do propose that this can be visually communicated on a single sheet of paper. If your organization has already done this, great! If your organization hasn't done this, then you'll have some additional work to do.

There are three actions for creating a strategy map: sort, sharpen, and structure.

Sort. First, you need to sort through all of the organizational goals and objectives to determine the universe of objectives that you are going to communicate to staff. If there is an objective that only pertains to the CEO, then you might choose to leave it off. Also, you want to sort through the layers of objectives and goals to determine the appropriate layer you wish to communicate. "Being the #1 organization in your industry" is too vague to be a tangible goal for most employees. "Re-organizing the human resources file cabinets" is probably too specific (and we hope it isn't on the list of organizational objectives). When you review the strategic plans of your organization, you are seeking to find those mid-level objectives that many employees will be working towards.

Some examples could be:

- Identify new clients
- Expand into new regions
- Reduce returns and rejections
- Increase satisfaction of those we serve

- Innovate new products and services
- Increase efficiency in our processes

It is likely that these will have specific measures. For example, they could read "Expand into two new regions" or "Increase customer satisfaction by five percent." Include these measures where they exist. These are helpful in communicating the intensity of the organizational objective.

Don't forget that there may be some ongoing objectives that don't get top billing, but they are equally important. Some organizations become so focused on the shiny new areas of innovation that they forget to articulate some foundational objectives. We think that most organizations would probably agree with something like these:

- Access accurate information quickly
- Adhere to efficient procedures
- Attract and retain competent staff

Whichever set of objectives you select, be sure to give them the 100 percent test. That is, can 100 percent of your employees have individual goals that would link to at least one of these organizational objectives? We typically look in two directions for this test: across the organization and down to the lowest level employee. Look across the organization to ensure that you have goals that speak to all departments from sales to operations to administrative support. Then, look down the organization chart to the most junior employee hired yesterday to ensure that this individual could link to one of the organizational objectives right now.

Sharpen. Now that you have your list of objectives, it's time to ensure that they have been translated from business jargon to everyday language. If your organization has already done this, great! If not, then you'll want to take a little time to craft the objectives into a similar tone and approachable language. Here's an example:

- Jargon: Increase capacity of online knowledge management practices to incorporate real-time sharing of emerging challenges and the access of relevant resources on the intranet to better enable staff performance
- Regular: Improve information sharing on the intranet

No doubt, we had a little fun in this example. Often, unfortunately, this example isn't too far from the truth. Work to distill the longer objective into a simple sentence. Find a balance so that the simple sentence is understood but not so vague that it is void of meaning.

When you present this list to the employees, we advise making the strategy document available so that people can see the entire goal and the rationale behind it. We find that creating a shorthand version makes it easier for people to recall and to select organizational objectives.

Structure. This is the last part of creating a strategy map. You'll want to structure these into a diagram or logical framework that organizes the objectives for the reader. If there are a few objectives, then this will be easy. With many, you may need to consider a way to group these various objectives if they aren't already organized.

Two examples are shown on the next page.

Strategy Map: Example #1

```
                          Vision
                          Mission

        External
        Objectives        Successful Projects
                          Responsible Growth
                          Technical Leadership

    Internal
    Competencies          Collaborate Worldwide
                     Access Accurate Information Quickly
                        Acquire and Develop Talent
                         Follow Efficient Procedures
```

Strategy Map: Example #2

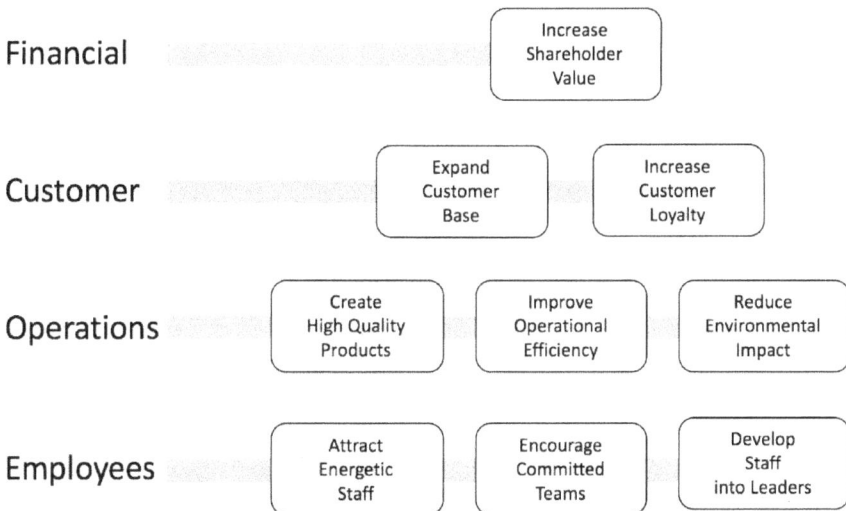

Financial		Increase Shareholder Value	
Customer	Expand Customer Base		Increase Customer Loyalty
Operations	Create High Quality Products	Improve Operational Efficiency	Reduce Environmental Impact
Employees	Attract Energetic Staff	Encourage Committed Teams	Develop Staff into Leaders

Step 2: Disseminate strategy map

The performance review shouldn't be the first time that employees are introduced to the organization's strategic goals. You'll want to ensure that there is a period of indoctrination and familiarization. Pursue whatever format or combination works best for your organization. A few examples are listed below:

- Staff meetings: Whether your organization has a series of smaller department meetings or organization wide meetings, use these opportunities to present the strategy map. Provide it at every meeting so that it is not a one-and-done presentation that is quickly forgotten.

- Video message: Video messaging is a great tool to personalize a message. You can reach everyone, and they can watch it multiple times or review certain segments, as necessary. A recorded voice-over embedded into a presentation slide can be created without additional technology tools.

- Posters: Placing posters in well-traveled areas such as the employee cafeteria is another way to help employees get familiar with the strategy map.

- C-suite updates: Review how the CEO and the other executives are communicating progress of the organization. Encourage them to use the strategy map that you have helped to create.

- Onboarding: We often become so focused on sharing new information with all existing employees that we forget to consider incoming employees. Include the strategy map as part of the onboarding for all new employees.

Step 3: Link goals to objectives

So far in this chapter, you have created (Step 1) and disseminated (Step 2) a strategy map. The purpose of these efforts is to increase the awareness and understanding of the strategic objectives by employees across the organization.

This is important for two reasons. First, employees should know what the organization is trying to attain so resources and actions can be better coordinated to achieve these objectives. The second reason is that employees derive a great amount of job satisfaction when they know that their work is contributing to the success of the organization.

Up to this point, every employee has completed the table listing the discipline goal and the measures. Hopefully, there are no more than two goals per employee. Each goal has about three measures. We're going to add a third column labeled **Link** as shown below.

Discipline Goal	Measures	Link
I will improve my ability to…		

What goes in this column? The employee will list the most relevant organizational objective from the strategy map. Whether you have an electronic performance management system or a paper-based process, you'll want to provide your strategy map with a numerical reference to all organizational objectives. The employee then lists the organizational objective to which their individual goal most closely contributes.

We encourage that you establish a practice of linking to only one (not multiple) objectives, even though an individual goal might contribute to both. We find that this provides a more thoughtful selection than choosing several objectives. Also, it will assist us with the last step of this chapter: aggregation.

Step 4: Aggregate links

After the performance reviews are completed, you can now aggregate a list of individual goals for each of the organizational objectives. Obviously, this is easier with an electronic system. You can manually compile this information into a simple spreadsheet with a paper-based system. This aggregation will allow you to achieve several tasks:

1. *Is there enough effort for each objective?* This is an important feedback loop to senior management. What if you set an organizational objective, but no one is working on it? That's exactly the information that you will be able to provide. You will be able to analyze the effort by department or skill level to ensure you have the right talent working on each organizational objective.

2. *What skill capacity needs are there?* As you look across the types of goals people have set as grouped by organizational objective, you will be able to see specific skill areas that may need support and talent development. This can inform the types of resources, training, and development activities you make available to employees.

3. *Are there staff that can be connected to collaborate on common items?* Finally, you can look at the clusters of individual goals to identify employees who could benefit by collaborating. Perhaps there are enough people to form a community of practice around a specific topic. Or, there might be an informal connection that could be facilitated by letting employees know others who are pursuing a similar goal.

This aggregation of links not only informs how people can collaborate, you can also use it as an early indicator on progress towards a company objective. If employees update the status of completion of their goals on a quarterly basis, you can see if there is a sustained effort towards a specific organizational objective. If employees are reporting low completion towards their individual goals, then it is likely that the organization will fail in reaching its objective. Reinforcement and supportive messages could then be delivered to staff. In this way, the human resources department becomes a critical partner in achieving objectives across the entire organization.

Additional Thoughts on Strategy Links

Consider creative formats, shapes, and images for designing the strategy map. Most strategies are a table or list of main objectives and sub-objectives. Explore other designs that clearly communicate the organizational objectives in an appealing manner.

Where appropriate, we also suggest paraphrasing organizational objectives into common language. Many organizations write their strategies to speak to a wider audience of stakeholders, and these strategy descriptions can become rather long and complicated sentences. Explore ways of re-writing these so that the essence is captured in a concise manner.

Ensure wide dissemination of the strategy map. Provide links to original strategy documents for those employees who wish to read the details behind the strategy map. Have appropriate people ready who can answer the intent and purpose of strategies. Be sure that the person implementing the performance review process (perhaps that's you) can explain all strategies.

The aggregation of strategy links is a powerful method of identifying where employees are focusing energy and potentially requiring support. Asking employees to update the status of completion of their discipline goals can also provide data when aggregated across the organization, or even just for a specific department.

Action Steps

☐ Create a strategy map

☐ Identify channels and venues for disseminating strategy map

☐ Incorporate strategy links on the review form

☐ Establish report format for aggregating discipline goals for each strategy (if possible, also establish quarterly or mid-year reporting on progress)

<u>Notes & Ideas</u>

Chapter 5: Upward Feedback

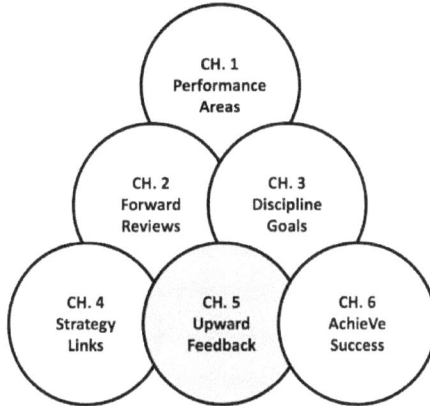

Collect meaningful information about supervisor performance

by engaging employees in a trusted feedback process.

Step 1	Define criteria
Step 2	Establish process
Step 3	Maintain integrity
Step 4	Identify trends

Why do we need upward reviews?

Take a moment to consider all the supervisors that you have had in your career. Think of the good supervisors. Think of the not-so-good supervisors. Okay, now ask yourself this: How often did you offer clear and constructive feedback to these supervisors?

You may have shown appreciation to the good supervisor, and you may have even told others about the joy in reporting to this supervisor. But did you ever sit with the supervisor and specifically articulate which of his or her behaviors contributed to your success? Did you describe how the supervisor might build on these strengths to further enhance your success?

And how about the not-so-good supervisor? Did you ever provide constructive feedback about his or her performance, and how that performance hindered your performance? Have you identified where this supervisor has demonstrated effective behaviors, however sporadic, and identified methods for increasing these behaviors? Or, like most of us, have you quietly grumbled about it or shared a few frustrating anecdotes with colleagues?

Now, you might say that this is the job of the supervisor's manager. (For simplicity sake, we'll refer to the employee, the supervisor, and the manager as three distinct roles: The employee reports to the supervisor, and the supervisor reports to the manager.) In this scenario, isn't it the responsibility of the manager to provide feedback to the supervisor?

Absolutely. But, in practical terms, how would the manager know what feedback to provide? Can the manager realistically know the impact of the supervisor's behavior on the employees? Surely there is some information (direct observation, staff turnover, department performance indicators) that the manager can review. However, this information is not likely to provide a complete picture of specific behaviors.

For this reason, it is difficult for the manager to give feedback on the performance area of supervision skills. After all, the manager of the supervisor doesn't have as much direct information as the employees. Could we solve this just by having the manager talk to the employees to get feedback for the supervisor?

No. First, employees – many who have not been supervisors themselves – may not be able to articulate their firsthand interactions into helpful information. Employees might use the opportunity to undermine the supervisor, or could be perceived as such by the supervisor.

Also, employees can fear retaliation. If an employee shares this information with a manager, how can the employee know that there will not be any retaliation from the supervisor? How can the organization protect itself from claims of retaliation after an employee shares unfavorable information?

Even if the organization were a completely open and trusting organization where managers could talk openly with employees about the supervisors without either the supervisor feeling undercut or the employees worrying about retaliation, what manager has the time to collect all this information?

A transparent and structured upward feedback process can support the supervisor, protect the confidentiality of the employee, and provide meaningful information to the manager. By having a transparent process, all staff understand how the information is being collected and shared. The supervisor knows how, when, and what information is being collected.

A structured process ensures that the right information is being collected from the employee in a helpful and easy manner. The structure also ensures that there is a firewall to protect the employees. And, a structured system enables aggregation of all employee feedback to identify areas of strengths and capacity building needs.

There are four steps to collecting upward feedback. This chapter will explain how to conduct these steps as summarized below:

Step 1: Define criteria	Select the behaviors expected from supervisors that represent organizational values.
Step 2: Establish process	Implement the steps to collect feedback about supervisors from employees.
Step 3: Maintain integrity	Establish mechanisms within the process to ensure confidentiality of participating employees.
Step 4: Identify trends	Identify the supervisor behaviors that need reinforcement and support across the organization.

Step 1: Define criteria

The first step is to define the criteria by which we are assessing supervisors. We are looking to define the specific behaviors that we expect to see in our supervisors. Similar to how we selected behaviors for our performance areas in chapter one, we will be identifying behaviors here. In fact, if you selected Supervision Skills as one of your performance areas, then pull that out.

Consider a supervisor. What do you expect the supervisor to do? We are looking for specific behaviors. "Supervisor motivates employee" is a bit vague. What does this look like? How do we know if this is happening? How would a supervisor know if he or she were engaged in this behavior?

Instead, "supervisor gives positive feedback when work is of high quality" is more specific. Also, "supervisor explains how my work contributes to larger organizational activities" and "supervisor gives me new and challenging work" are also more specific. All three of these statements could be considered behaviors that motivate an employee. For this reason, we must ensure that we are identifying specific behaviors to know if supervisors are performing to the standards and culture of our organization.

If you could film every interaction a supervisor had with an employee, you would be able to identify behaviors. All behaviors are descriptive. An example of what <u>not</u> to write would be "supervisor has the best interests of the employee in mind when making decisions." How would you ever see this? Instead, we could try this one: "supervisor solicits input from employees on decisions that affect them." This is something that you could observe.

Here's another example: "supervisor maintains a positive work environment." Is that specific? Would you be able to observe it? No, probably not. More specific behaviors under this might be "supervisor facilitates discussions to ensure that all employees are heard" or "supervisor publicly acknowledges the successful contributions of employees." These are specific behaviors.

It is important that you take the time to identify the behaviors that your organization expects from your supervisors. It should be a behavior that any supervisor or employee could put into practice without having to interpret the meaning. Motivate an employee? There are whole books on this. "Supervisor gives positive feedback when work is of high quality" requires no further analysis.

Identify behaviors that reflect your desired culture and organizational values. Consider behaviors that are core to your values, even if they are already widely practiced. Cementing these values into behaviors will keep them relevant as new supervisors join the organization. Also, identify behaviors that are not yet commonly practiced, but you find vital to achieve the organizational objectives. Review the behaviors identified in the Supervision Skills performance area (if selected). Let supervisors know that these are the behaviors to which they will be assessed.

How many behaviors? We created twenty-two discreet behaviors at ACDI/VOCA. They are more specific than the behaviors identified in chapter one. Our best advice is to focus on the specific behaviors you want to measure, and stop when you have identified them. If you are stuck after only seven behaviors, you may be not getting specific enough.

Here are some examples we use in our organization:

- Demonstrates to me the importance of maintaining good relationships with other departments
- Recognizes and reinforces what I do well
- Keeps me informed of the bigger picture
- Communicates expectations clearly

Step 2: Establish process

With the criteria defined, it is now time to collect input from the employees. Employees, after all, have the best vantage point for seeing if the supervisor is practicing the list of behaviors on a consistent basis. We encourage employees to fill out an upward review for their supervisor and for anyone else in their reporting line. For example, an employee can complete an upward review on the immediate supervisor, the manager of that supervisor, and the manager of that manager all the way up to the CEO.

Obviously, the employee is going to have less and less firsthand knowledge as we go up the organizational chart. Some expectations would change the further from direct supervision the employee is from the manager being reviewed. That's okay. The employee does not have to evaluate every single behavior of the supervisors or managers. Perhaps there is one behavior that the employee wants to highlight for managers far removed from routine contact with the employee.

We also require employees to sign their names to upward reviews. This is a critical step of ownership. Although we maintain the confidentiality of the employee (explained below), requiring a name avoids several potential issues. First, having an employee sign a name avoids "ballot-box stuffing," wherein an employee might try to generate a perception of mass indignation (or praise) for a supervisor. It also increases the accuracy of what is written and diminishes snarky comments and information heard second hand.

How do we collect input from employees in a way that can provide meaningful analysis of these behaviors while making it easy for employees to give feedback? How do we balance this need for both ease and depth?

First, let's consider what we want to know from employees. Most supervisors, even the worst, practice most of the behaviors occasionally. Asking an employee to indicate if this behavior is performed is not helpful. Also, providing an open entry process puts too much pressure on the employee (who may not have ever been a supervisor) to provide clear and helpful feedback.

We're looking to get feedback on the frequency of these behaviors. The organization has identified the desired behaviors that are believed to reflect the culture of the organization and will contribute to the performance of the organization. Let's see what frequency in which these behaviors are performed. That would be helpful feedback to give a supervisor, right?

Never does this	Sometimes does this	Does this about half the time	Does this most of the time	Always does this	N/A

In this table, there is a range from *Never does this* to *Always does this.* There's an option for N/A if the employee believes the behavior is irrelevant for her situation; for example, if the employee is evaluating her supervisor's manager who may not be assigned some of the direct supervision responsibilities. We also provide a comment box for each behavior.

Hold on – aren't these ratings? What are we doing here? In this instance, we are simply asking employees to indicate the frequency in which something happens. They can provide specific and detailed feedback through the comment boxes. No score or specific comments will be passed on the supervisor in the final review. The upward review is a checklist for the employee to indicate if the behaviors that the organization has deemed necessary are regularly occurring.

On a side note, there was a positive consequence to sharing the list of behaviors with supervisors. One of the behaviors we introduced was "my supervisor encourages me to participate in company-wide activities." For our organization, it was not that supervisors were discouraging participation, it was that they were not actively encouraging it. They just assumed that employees would attend those events. New employees were unsure if they should attend; so low turnout and missed opportunities for employees to connect frequently occurred. After introducing the list and communicating to supervisors the importance of encouraging employees to be involved in these activities, we saw a sharp increase in attendance to events. Employees confirmed that supervisors were encouraging them to attend these events during the next round of upward reviews.

Prepare the upward feedback form, and send it out to employees. However, you will need to protect the confidentiality of the process. For this, let's read the next step: *Maintain integrity.*

Step 3: Maintain integrity

A supervisor documenting feedback on an employee is a sensitive topic. When an employee is providing feedback on a supervisor, it can be even more sensitive. There is a power differential that needs to be recognized. The employee's concern of retaliation, whether perceived or actual, needs to be mitigated. Maintaining the integrity of the process is very important.

This is where a trusted facilitator comes in. Typically, this is someone in human resources. Completed upward review forms are submitted to this facilitator. The facilitator compiles the review forms for each supervisor. The facilitator then writes a summary of the feedback on each supervisor reviewed. This summary contains no information that can be attributed back to a specific employee.

This summary is then given to the manager of the supervisor. Remember, this information is being compiled to help the manager of the supervisor provide constructive feedback. The manager does not need every bit of detail, just enough information from the employees to provide helpful feedback. The facilitator provides a summary to the manager.

For the summary report, the facilitator selects a handful of behaviors to reinforce or strengthen the supervisor's performance. If you have identified approximately twenty behaviors, you do not provide a summary report on all twenty behaviors to the manager. You provide the highlights. These would include a few areas in which the supervisor is not practicing a behavior, and a few areas in which the supervisor is demonstrating the behavior frequently.

It is a bit of a judgment call, but your goal is to help provide the data that the manager can combine with his or her own observations. The combination of this data and direct observations will then be used by the manager to complete the *Now+Next* boxes under the category of *Supervisory Skills* or whichever performance area you have designated for feedback on supervisory skills.

What if there are only one or two employees that report to a supervisor? Won't it be obvious who sent the feedback about the supervisor? There may be situations when you only receive an upward review from one or two employees on a specific supervisor; or, the supervisor might only have one employee. If there are multiple employees who haven't submitted an upward review, a gentle nudge and encouragement to these employees will help provide more information.

In the case of only one employee reporting to the supervisor, then you'll need to craft the summary in broader language. The supervisor appears to be doing these items well (and make your list of a few), and please consider if the supervisor should spend more time doing these other items (and make a list of a few). The manager will need to supplement the upward review with personal observations and other feedback received. A survey size of one upward review is not enough information to draw substantial conclusions. The manager should be encouraged to find additional sources before drawing conclusions.

We have been asked about whether to use a paper or online system. We have conducted the upward review and collected responses with both a paper based system and online system. For either system, the employee responses still come to human resources and are not released directly to the supervisor. Even with an automated online system, the summary is still created manually by human resources. This summary is the only document given to the manager.

There is the need to communicate protection and confidentiality on behalf of the employees in order to get the best feedback. The goal is to ensure that employees feel confident that their individual responses will not be extracted from the system and attributed to them by their supervisors. Even though most of the responses are positive, the integrity of the system depends on anonymity.

Step 4: Identify trends

You've aggregated results for each supervisor. Now, let's aggregate the data across all supervisors to group all behaviors (not supervisors) into three groups: those behaviors that are consistently being performed, behaviors being moderately performed, and those behaviors not being performed consistently. With this information, you can act on the three groups of behaviors.

For those actions being performed consistently, watch the trend for a couple of years or performance cycles. If they are core behaviors that are central to the values of the organization, then continue surveying on these behaviors to ensure that supervisors stay consistent. Remember, the questions serve a dual purpose—to facilitate feedback and provide a tool for supervisors to use as a checklist of desired behaviors for your organization.

For behaviors being moderately performed, consider any reinforcement that you can provide to encourage these behaviors. They aren't a problem, but they aren't consistent either. You might select a couple of good examples of these behaviors and amplify them across the organization to encourage others to adopt these practices. Seeking positive examples is a good way to encourage others to practice a desired behavior.

For those behaviors not being performed, you'll need to check for barriers, confirm understanding, and then issue explicit communications. First, evaluate if there are any barriers to practicing this behavior or a negative incentive for practicing these behaviors. For example, you might have an expected behavior that supervisors encourage staff to participate in organization-wide events, but the supervisors are given a bonus based on the amount of billable hours their staff charge to clients. This is a barrier, and you will have a difficult time in changing their behavior. Another example of a barrier would be that you expect supervisors to give training opportunities to staff, but there is no budget for training. Employees will rate this as a behavior that doesn't happen often, but there is a barrier that keeps the supervisor from performing this behavior.

After you have ensured that there are no significant barriers hindering adoption of these behaviors, reach out to a few managers. Speak with them about the behavior to ascertain the reasons why it isn't happening. If the consensus is a lack of skill, then consider some form of training or capacity building. If there is no discernible barrier to the desired conduct, then you'll need to issue explicit communications to supervisors. Explain the importance of practicing the desired behavior and ask the managers for reinforcement.

As you conduct interventions in the three categories of behaviors, you can compare survey results against prior years to see which behaviors are responding to your interventions. You should share this with senior management to acquire additional resources to conduct your development activities.

Additional Thoughts on Upward Reviews

The most important component of a successful upward feedback process is naming a trusted facilitator. Be sure to select someone who is in a role that is appropriate for this type of activity. Also, ensure that this person is well-trusted and has a solid track record of handling confidential information carefully.

Watch carefully over the process for the first two cycles to ensure that employee contributions are kept confidential and that source information is not shared with managers or supervisors. Quickly respond to any actual or perceived actions that might undermine confidence in the process.

As for the behaviors – and we can't stress this enough – be sure that they pass the visibility test. They need to be behaviors that can be observed and described without interpretation. Review each of these carefully to ensure that they are behaviors. Ensure that there is consensus across the leaders of the organization for the selected behaviors. And, remind senior leaders that all lower level supervisors and employees will be watching for senior leaders to model the behaviors.

Align training activities with the aggregation of upward feedback data. The frequency of supervisor behaviors can serve as an important baseline for measuring changes in behavior after any capacity building activities. Reviewing the aggregation of behavior frequency year over year can help to focus limited staff development resources and demonstrate their impact.

Action Steps

☐   Define specific behaviors for supervisors

☐   Create the upward review form and process

☐   Determine the trusted facilitator

☐   Establish report format for aggregating all feedback

<u>Notes & Ideas</u>

Chapter 6: AchieVe Success

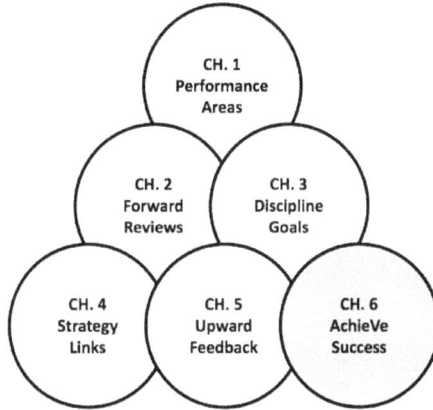

Put into operation the core elements

of the AchieVe performance management system.

Step 1	Create review form
Step 2	Establish quality control
Step 3	Support meaningful dialogue
Step 4	Define follow-up schedule

How do we ensure AchieVe success?

Over the last five chapters, we have covered a lot of concepts. We started by defining Performance Areas (chapter one) and then using Forward Reviews (chapter two) to provide clear feedback and guidance.

We created Meaningful Goals (chapter three) that were connected to organizational objectives with Strategy Links (chapter four). As supervision is a critical skill in which much of the performance information is collected by the employees, we established an avenue for employees to share their observations with Upward Feedback (chapter five).

Like any new set of knowledge, it is only useful if we can put it into action. We can read the rules of the road and study the inside of a vehicle for only so long. Eventually, you've got to start the engine and take the car out for a drive.

In this chapter, we give you the keys. Time to take this for a spin!

To successfully navigate your performance review process to arrive at the destination of AchieVe success, consider these four elements: the lines on the road, the stoplight, the dialogue, and a schedule. (If we're going to have a car analogy, we might as well have a little fun with it.)

First, the lines on the road. Just as there are lines on the road to successfully guide traffic, you'll need a simple performance review form that guides both employees and supervisors. We'll provide a template in this chapter for you to revise to the needs of your organization.

Next, you need a stoplight. You want the supervisors to stop for a moment after writing the review – and before meeting with the employee – to ensure that what they have written accurately and clearly articulates what they intended to say. You'll need to determine who will perform the role of the stoplight to ensure the quality and integrity of your performance review system.

Just as there needs to be clear communication between the co-pilot and the driver, there needs to be clear communications between supervisor and employee. This is the critical moment of the entire performance review process. Providing guidance to supervisors prior to the meeting will be a critical factor of AchieVe success.

Finally, just as a vehicle has a schedule of routine maintenance, your performance system will have a schedule of routine activities to support the progress of employees towards their discipline goals.

Putting the car analogy aside, this chapter covers four critical actions that will help you to successfully launch and sustain the performance review process. These steps are summarized below:

Step 1: Create review form	Assemble the components of the review form in a simple but thorough template.
Step 2: Establish quality control	Identify individuals and methods for ensuring clear and effective content in review forms.
Step 3: Support meaningful dialogue	Provide specific guidance to supervisors to improve the dialogue with employees.
Step 4: Define follow-up schedule	Define and schedule specific activities to help employees strive towards discipline goals.

Step 1: Create review form

Let's create your performance review form. You'll see from the example below that there are five sections.

- Section A – Performance Areas

In chapter one, you defined performance areas. For each performance area you defined specific behaviors. In chapter two, you used *Now+Next* boxes to format the forward looking review. These two elements are combined into Section A. For each performance area identified, list a pair of *Now+Next* boxes. Be sure to mark those performance areas that are required and those that depend on position (such as Supervision Skills). Also, be sure to provide access (either in paper form or through an online link) to the full list of behaviors for each performance area.

Knowledge & Skills	
NOW	**NEXT**

Job Performance	
NOW	**NEXT**

Professional Relationships	
NOW	**NEXT**

Teamwork	
NOW	**NEXT**

Supervision Skills (supervisors only)	
NOW	**NEXT**

- Section B – Previous Goals

In chapter three, you learned about discipline goals and the emphasis on reviewing past goals. In this section of the review, provide a box for each goal. We've listed three boxes here to indicate discipline, measures, and performance. **Discipline Goal** is the "improve my ability to" statement. **Measures** are the tangible measures that were to be used to assess progress on that discipline. **Performance** is where you evaluate performance against the measures, including any external factors that helped or hindered. Consider adding additional reflection questions as described in chapter three. We've made room for only two discipline goals on the form, as we think two are enough. You will decide how many to allow on your form.

PREVIOUS GOALS		
Discipline Goal	**Measures**	**Performance**

- Section C – Summary

When reviewing the performance areas of Section A and the performance against previous goals in Section B, there should be a story that emerges about the overall performance. Summarize that story in this section. The first paragraph describes the year in review and the second paragraph describes what the employee should be focusing on during the next review period.

SUMMARY

- Section D – Discipline Goals

Now we define goals for the year ahead. In chapter three, you learned about discipline goals. In chapter four, you learned about linking these discipline goals to organizational objectives. The discipline goals and their links to organizational objectives are collected here in Section D of the performance review. We've listed three boxes here to indicate discipline goal, measures, and link. **Discipline Goal** is the "improve my ability to" statement. The **Measures** are the tangible measures that will be used to assess progress on that discipline goal. The **Link** is for the relevant organizational objective as indicated on your strategy map. We've made room for only two discipline goals on the form as we think two are enough. You'll decide how many to allow on your form.

DISCIPLINE GOALS		
Discipline Goal	**Measures**	**Link**

- Section E Employee Comments, and Signatures of Supervisor and Employee

The last section of the review is for employee comments. After the employee meets with the supervisor, the review form is presented to the employee for any comments. Comments are optional. The signature does not indicate that the employee agrees with everything written in the performance review, only that the employee has received the performance review.

EMPLOYEE COMMENTS

Employee Signature: _____

Supervisor Signature: _____

Step 2: Establish quality control

After a supervisor completes the review form as described in Step 1, you'll want to ensure a quality control check prior to having the employee see it. This is especially important in the beginning when you first switch to this process. Supervisors are learning a new process and will benefit from having feedback on the actual reviews. You'll also reduce the number of awkward review meetings by ensuring that reviews are accurately communicating what is intended by the supervisor.

Supervisors approach review writing differently. Some are very explicit and leave little vagueness. Many supervisors are vague in their writing, particularly as they are trying to give constructive feedback. Sometimes, the sentences can get so convoluted that employees believe they are being corrected, not praised.

That's why a quality control point is important. You'll want this neutral facilitator to read each review to ensure that there is a consistency through the entire form: From the performance areas to last year's goals and to this year's goals, making sure the language is clear.

Also, double check that the goals are discipline goals. As we explained in chapter three, this will be one of the most difficult transitions as supervisors tend to think in active tasks and not in long-term disciplines. Supervisors tend to think of the specifics that they want the employee to perform. Helping them to frame these tasks within the broader discipline goal will benefit both them and the employee. Finally, check that each discipline goal is linked to an organizational objective.

Be sure that there are no surprises in the review. The supervisor should not introduce an entire area of poor performance that has not been shared with the employee until the performance review. If you discover this in the review, meet with the supervisor to discuss how to address it. Perhaps the performance review can introduce the topic, but then you will need to work with the supervisor to establish a consistent process of monitoring, support, and – if needed – corrective action. The performance review should not be the first intervention for corrective action.

Step 3: Support meaningful dialogue

The format of the performance review and the structured process in crafting the performance review leads to a meaningful conversation between the supervisor and employee. With clear *Now+Next* statements, they can discuss and analyze specific incidents as demonstrations of critical behaviors. They can identify specific opportunities to perform higher level aspects of these behaviors. Discipline goals shape the year as an exciting opportunity to not only contribute to organizational objectives, but to gain valuable experience for one's career and profession.

Even with the structured format, consider providing guidance to supervisors about conducting the review meeting. A few tips to share could include staying focused on observations, steering clear of salary discussions, and avoiding surprises. Let's take a closer look at these tips.

As human beings, we tend to summarize observable actions into abstract characteristics. If my neighbor continually shouts at children for walking on his lawn, then I might summarize him as being grumpy. However, grumpy is not an observable state of mind. Shouting at children is observable.

When supervisors talk with employees, they need to describe observable behaviors and avoid characteristics. For example, supervisors can discuss how well (or not) employees communicate with clients, but they should avoid using terms like introverted or outgoing. Supervisors can describe how employees check for accuracy and review documents for quality, but should avoid using terms such as sloppy or nit-picky. By staying focused on behaviors, the discussion can be an open dialogue about how these behaviors do (or don't) contribute to the success of the department and organization.

A topic that often arises in performance reviews is compensation. This topic should stay completely outside of the performance review dialogue. Any sentences spoken about performance areas, critical behaviors, and discipline goals will not be truly heard. Instead, the employee will be waiting to get past those deeper development topics to get to the here and now of compensation. Compensation is important, but the discussion should take place separately outside of the feedback session on performance.

Ultimately, compensation is not what sustains higher performance. Motivation comes from challenging work and meaningful contribution. The topic of motivation falls outside of this book. If you are interested in the topic, we highly recommend you read Daniel Pink's book *Drive: The Surprising Truth about What Motivates Us* (Pink, 2009). It may help to explain our view that the compensation topic should be separated from the meaningful dialogue about performance, growth, and contribution to organizational objectives. You can also find a ten minute video on YouTube that was adapted from his talk at the RSA.

Finally, to risk repetition, there should be no surprises in the performance review session. As explained above in Step 2, the review session should not introduce areas of poor performance. The supervisor and human resources should meet to discuss a strategy for addressing these behaviors.

Step 4: Define follow-up schedule

After the flurry of annual performance reviews – writing self-assessments, collecting upward feedback, writing discipline goals, conducting dialogues, and identifying linked goal trends – what happens next? Well, often there is a push to return to normal. That is, everything gets filed and too often forgotten.

In this step, we'll work on a schedule of activities that you can conduct throughout the year to encourage supervisors and employees to stay focused on these critical items. We all need reminders and encouragement to stay atop our goals. Here are a series of activities that we have found helpful in keeping staff on track.

Most of our messaging is directed to the employee. The employee is ultimately responsible for the growth and progress of her own career. Yes, the supervisor plays an important part, but we don't want the employee to become stagnant in waiting for a supervisor to define a way forward. We want our employees to show initiative and to be an active driver of her own career.

- Self-check (quarterly). Once a quarter, send an email to staff encouraging them to pull out their discipline goals and to review them. Are they making progress? What are the next three actions they can take right now to move towards their discipline goals? Encourage them to talk with their supervisor if they see an opportunity within their department to benefit the department and work towards their discipline goals.

  At this time, ask employees to update the status on their goals. There are different ways of doing this. They can indicate with a percentage completed for each measure or at a stage level completed (not started, partially done, halfway, mostly done, achieved). This is a self-check for the employee, and it will contribute to the trend report (described below).

- Trend report (quarterly). If you encourage employees to conduct a review of their discipline goals quarterly and update their achievement status (as explained above), then you will have an opportunity to aggregate this information into two helpful reports: department and organization.

  For each department, you can aggregate the information to see how well the staff of each department are progressing on their goals. This can be helpful feedback to give to a supervisor. A supervisor can communicate with employees and help to support progress on these goals. At the end of the year, this is also helpful feedback for the manager writing the supervisor's review.

  At an organization level, you can review the progress of discipline goals as linked to organizational objectives. This can provide an additional data point to senior management as towards the overall progress towards these objectives. Senior management can choose to increase communications, support, or follow-up on initiatives to encourage and manage progress towards these objectives. It also reminds senior management of the importance of the entire performance management system. It shows the linkage of performance reviews to critical organizational strategies, and that it is not a one-time event.

- Check-in (mid-year). Here, we ask the supervisors to actively review the progress of employees towards their goals. It is not a formal documented meeting, unless there is a performance issue that needs to be addressed. But again, hopefully performance issues have been addressed during the flow of work and not held until such a check-in. It is at least an opportunity to raise such issues if they haven't been addressed until now.

For the supervisor, it is an opportunity to identify specific opportunities in which the employee can engage to achieve the discipline goals. And in some cases, it is a chance to amend the measures (but not the discipline goals themselves) if circumstances have changed dramatically since the writing of the performance review and discipline goals.

Additional Thoughts on AchieVe Success

There's the old question: "How do you eat an elephant?" The simple answer is "one bite at a time." And so it is with installing your AchieVe performance system. It might seem like a lot, but it can be done one bite at a time.

First, get leadership on board. If you have not already been assigned to revamp your performance management system, obtain agreement that it is a worthwhile endeavor. Next, get consensus with leadership on what you want out of your performance evaluation process. Don't get into specifics of what it should look like, or you will get as many opinions as there are people in the room.

Remember the four "R's" we discussed in the introduction? Reach, Realize, Reinforce, and Retain. Use that framework or something that works for you to get everyone on the same page. Obtain agreement from leadership that if you produce a system that produces the results you agree are needed, then they will support it. Don't forget to remind them of this when you present the final product.

You don't have to do it alone. We strongly encourage you to consider using an Advisory Council. An Advisory Council is roughly eight to ten people from across the organization. Their role is to provide advice. You do, they react.

Now, you might be wondering how this reduces your workload if you are still doing all the work and they are only reacting. By working through an Advisory Council, you will likely have a more thorough system with less resistance and more support during the implementation phase.

You have the advantage of gathering comments and insights from staff. Draft your list of performance areas and the Advisory Council confirms or suggests adjustments to the list. Present your strategy map, and let the Advisory Council suggest changes. Share your list of upward review questions, and the Advisory Council can help to identify any missing behaviors.

With an Advisory Council, you get the confidence of having a thoroughly vetted system. Also, you are providing this group the opportunity to become familiar with the upcoming changes. This provides additional credibility and outreach when you can explain to departments and staff that a cross-organizational Advisory Council helped to construct critical elements of the system.

So, don't go it alone or keep it within your department. Engage staff across the organization on your Advisory Council. With collaboration, you will be well on your way to creating a performance system that reaches organizational goals, realizes individual goals, reinforces core values, and retains critical skills.

Action Steps

☐ Create the review form with the five sections

☐ Identify and train people who will act as quality control

☐ Provide guidelines to supervisors for meaningful dialogue

☐ Define a follow-up schedule

Notes & Ideas

www.ingramcontent.com/pod-product-compliance
Lightning Source LLC
Chambersburg PA
CBHW060037210326
41520CB00009B/1170